DISCARDED

The Hispanic Presence in Florida

The Hispanic Presence in Florida

Edited by José Agustín Balseiro

with contributions by
Vicente Murga, R. S. Boggs, W. C. Arnade,
William M. Straight, Rosa M. Abella,
Carlos Ripoll, and Antonio Jorge.

E. A. SEEMANN PUBLISHING, INC.

Library of Congress Cataloging in Publication Data
Main entry under title:

The Hispanic presence in Florida.

Bibliography: p.
Includes index.
1. Spanish Americans in Florida--Addresses, essays, lectures. 2. Refugees--Florida--Addresses, essays, lectures. 3. Refugees--Cuba--Addresses, essays, lectures. 4. Florida--History--Addresses, essays, lectures. I. Balseiro, Jose Austin, 1900- II. Murga Sanz, Vicente.
F320.S75H57   975.9'004'68   76-57968
ISBN 0-912458-82-8
ISBN 0-912458-83-6 pbk.

Copyright © 1976 by Jose Agustin Balseiro
ISBN: 0-912458-82-8 (cloth), 0-912458-83-8 (paperback)
Library of Congress Catalog Card Number: 76-57968

All rights reserved, including rights of reproduction and use in any form or by any means, including the making of copies by any photo process, or by any electronic or mechanical device, printed or written or oral, or recording for use in any knowledge or retrieval system or device, unless permission in writing is obtained from the copyright proprietors.

Manufactured in the United States of America.

*To the memory of
Mercedes,
so devotedly
involved in the
publication of
this book.*

Nov. 28, 1976

CONTENTS

General Introduction / 9
  by José Agustín Balseiro
"Florida" So Named by Ponce de León / 33
  by Vicente Murga
Mosaic of Traditional Culture / 61
  by R.S. Boggs
Medicine in Spanish Florida / 77
  by William M. Straight, M.D.
Florida During the American Revolutionary War / 95
  by Charles W. Arnade
José Martí and the American Founding Fathers / 123
  by Carlos Ripoll
The Cultural Presence of the Cuban Exile in Miami / 133
  by Rosa M. Abella
Characteristics and Consequences / 141
  by Antonio Jorge
Index / 157

GENERAL INTRODUCTION
by
José Agustín Balseiro

It was the mayor of Miami, Maurice A. Ferré, who originated the idea for this book, and it was he who suggested that I should be charged with its organization. The project received the unanimous approval of the Hispanic-American Committee for the Bicentennial Celebration of the Independence of the Thirteen North American Colonies, Third Century, U.S.A. I do not doubt that the mayor's suggestion was greatly influenced by the facts that we are both Puerto Ricans, that we have been residents of Florida for more than a quarter of a century, and that Miami, together with Boston, New York, and Philadelphia, is one of the four cities honored by the government of the United States to represent the nation in this celebration.

If the mayor and myself have always felt pride in Puerto Rico, in this present endeavor our pride in our birthplace is increased. For it was indeed from Puerto Rico in 1513 that Juan Ponce de León, the first governor of our island, set sail for the territory that would come to be called the United States, thus bringing about the initial contact between the Old World and the mainland of North America. On a later trip in 1521, Ponce de León was gravely wounded by the natives and taken to Havana. Eventually, his remains were transferred to their permanent resting place in the cathedral of San Juan, Puerto Rico.

In September 1565, after having previously stopped in Puerto Rico, Don Pedro Menéndez de Avilés arrived at the future site of Misión del

---
*English translation by Piedad Ferrer Robertson.

Nombre de Dios (Mission of the Name of God) in Florida. Two years later he arrived in Miami. Thus was sealed the long and close historical relationship between the smallest of the islands of the Greater Antilles and the semitropical peninsula where the United States ends, embraced by the keys and bathed by the ocean waters. The most important of the keys, the Cayo Hueso (Key West) of Martí and the Cuban cigar makers, has been, in the second half of the twentieth century, a hand stretched out to rescue the victims of tyranny. Hundreds of thousands have recovered once more, in Florida, a heroic will to live. Their initiative, their creativeness, and their courage, so many times tested, brought a new strength that has enriched not only the Hispanic-Americans residing in Miami, but also the city's North American residents.

Here, the newcomers found that the University of Miami opened its arms to their doctors, lawyers, and librarians. In our auditoriums, some of the most famous of Hispanic-American virtuosi and musical composers have been heard. On the twelfth of February 1954, for example, in the presence of Heitor Villa-Lobos, I delivered a lecture on the personality and work of this great composer. (Later I was able to repeat my dissertation in his own Brazil and in several Spanish cities, accompanied by the Puerto Rican concert pianist Jesús María Sanromá.) On the fourteenth and fifteenth of that same February, Villa-Lobos, the composer of *Momoprecóce,* conducted a program of his own music. He was at that time granted the degree of Doctor of Music by the University of Miami as well as on several occasions by other universities in the United States.

Among the representatives of the Hispanic music world that have been heard in Miami are: Victoria de los Angeles, Graciela Rivera, Claudio Arrau, Andrés Segovia, José Iturbi and his sister Amparo, Jesús María Sanromá, Jaime Laredo, the Bolet brothers, and the Figueroa Quintet. Not easily forgotten was the *Malagueña* of Ernesto Lecuona and the Puerto Rican composer Rafael Balseiro's *El Niágara,* well interpreted by the University of Miami Symphony Orchestra.

The association goes further. Ernest Hemingway resided in Key West and in Cuba. His love for Cuba and its people was immortalized in *The Old Man and the Sea,* as previously his love for Spain had found expression in *Death in the Afternoon* and in *For Whom the Bell Tolls.*

Many Hispanic-American youths came to Florida attracted by its colleges and universities in cities like Miami, Gainesville, Tallahassee, Tampa, and Pensacola; and some attended other schools in the Sunshine State. Dr. José Antonio Dávila, the author of *Vendimia* (San Juan, 1940),

General Introduction [11]

one of the best contemporary neoromantic poets, was one of those that came to Florida. He had graduated from Jefferson Medical College in Philadelphia and interned at the Duval County Hospital. He practiced medicine in Orlando. The oranges, grapefruits, and limes of that citrus region and the brightness of the skies must have reminded him of our native Puerto Rico to which he returned later and where he died.[1]

The theme of Florida seems to have attracted the early Spanish writers as well as the peninsula itself attracted the explorers. *"Florida"* is the title given to a poem of Alonso Gregorio Escobedo; and Father Jerónimo de Oré wrote about these lands in his chronicles of the New World.

Spanish Colonial Florida was the subject of one of the books of "the *Inca,"* Garcilaso de la Vega, in 1605. The Florida of "the *Inca"* is the result of the tales told by one of Hernando de Soto's companions to his friend Garcilaso. It was Hernando de Soto, with the title of Governor of Florida and Cuba, who had discovered Tampa Bay towards the end of May in 1539 and Pensacola Bay shortly thereafter. Governor de Soto participated in the conquest of Perú and explored some lands of Central America before arriving, in May two years later, at the banks of the Mississippi River. Garcilaso, related to the exquisite sixteenth-century poet of the same name ("Clear, serene eyes"), was able to transmit onto paper the excitement and high adventure that these men lived. "The *Inca,"* Garcilaso, with his double heritage, brought together in his work the sensitivity, the fantasy, and the knowledge of the indiginous Peruvian and the Spanish cultures in what he called, "the flower of Spain."

In 1693, three years after publishing his book, *Los infortunios que Alonso Ramírez, natural de la ciudad de San Juan de Puerto Rico, padeció (The Unfortunate Happenings of Alonso Ramírez, Native of the City of San Juan, Puerto Rico),* Carlos de Sigüenza y Góngora was commissioned by the viceroy of New Spain, Don Gasper de la Cerda Sandoval y Mendoza, to take a scientific expedition to Pensacola *(Panzacola),* which was at the time the capital of West Florida.

Zenobia Camprubí and her world-famous husband, Juan Ramón Jiménez, have been guests of the University of Miami. Years later, while living in Puerto Rico, Juan Ramón Jiménez would be awarded the Nobel Prize for Literature (1956). I mentioned Zenobia's name first not out of

---

[1] See José Agustín Balseiro, *Expresión de Hispanoamérica,* vol. I, second edition (Madrid: Gredos, 1970), pp. 247-261.

courtesy to a woman. I once told a South American reporter that if I were to write a book about Juan Ramón, out of every hundred pages seventy-five would be about her and twenty-five about him. Such was the human quality, the spiritual nobility, the understanding of the wife of this psychologically complex man, the immortal author of *Animal de Fondo*. Not least among his idiosyncrasies, Zenobia had to contend with his preoccupation with immortality. Those of us who knew Juan Ramón and have read him in depth are well aware of the care and anguish which he lavished on the projection of his future image.

In Coral Gables, which is part of metropolitan Miami, Juan Ramón wrote a lyrical remembrance of his life between 1939 and 1942. It consists of some nine pieces which make no direct mention of the city, but which offer here and there a slight suggestion:

> The sea again, the sea
> with me.

An opening remark:

> The palm caresses the pine
> with moist air;

Romances de Coral Gables (Mexico, 1948) indicates the mental state of a poet who, far away from his homeland, lives accompanied by his melancholy:

> But the loneliness is here,
> But faith cannot be changed.
> For that which was external,
> Is found now only in the soul.

He gave a copy of this book to my wife and myself when Jiménez and I were teaching in the summer program at Duke. In it he wrote, "To my dear Balseiros, from a friend who doesn't forget them, Juan Ramón." (The words were written in that peculiar handwriting of his which reminds one of Arabic signs.) We had met in Madrid two decades before our Duke encounter. On both occasions I was able to confirm, together with my admiration for his lyric perfectionism and his desire to excel all of his contemporaries, that his character was a mixture of the angelic and the diabolic. When he would talk about some writer for whom he expressed admiration, his words had the sharpness of a scalpel cutting into the flesh in search of infection and revealing the disease with a morbid insistency: Menéndez Pidal, Antonio Machado, Pedro Salinas, Federico García Lorca, Pablo Neruda—no one escaped him. Publicly, at times, he would rectify or justify his remarks and would express other opinions.

General Introduction [13]

Juan Ramón had been obsessed by the idea of death since adolescence. In the fourth part of *Questions to the Resident* (Romance No. 6) he has the following question, so significant to an exile:

> Do you with pleasure wait here
> For the death of your tomorrow?
> Is it possible from here to
> Also depart to a homeless eternity?

Among others that came as guests to the University of Miami in the forties was Américo Castro, the great Spanish scholar. We were to travel together to Havana to deliver lectures at the International Institute of Iberoamerican Literature.

And how can one forget that Gabriela Mistral, the 1945 Nobel Prize laureate, had wanted to live in Coral Gables? Unfortunately, she did not stay here long. Shortly after her arrival, she received a cable from Carlos Ibáñez, then president of Chile, asking her to join the Chilean representatives at the United Nations. How unhappy she was at having to leave "such a pleasant environment" so soon. Together we reminisced about Puerto Rico which she had so lovingly written about:

> So sweet of speech
> Like a child;
> Blessed to sing
> Like a hosanna.

She mentioned again and again the tasty foods of my island homeland. She had particularly enjoyed the *alcapurrias.* On the following day, the morning of her departure for the north, I took her a platter full of *alcapurrias* which had been prepared by Mrs. Balseiro. Gabriela delightedly thanked me.

Another brief but important visitor was the effusive Asturian Alfonso Camín, whom I had met in Spain some years before. One day I received a letter from Mexico in which he informed me that he would stop in Miami on his way to Puerto Rico. At the airport where I met him, he asked me to drive him through the city and Dade County, for he wanted to see as much as possible of the entire area. He looked eagerly at everything. He commented enthusiastically on all that he saw, mixing his comments on modern Miami with a hearty discourse on the past of Spain, defending the greatness of Philip II over that of his father, Charles I.

In 1956, he sent me a book, *With the Rhythm of the Water* (Songs of Courtship). On page 287 I found a poem called "A Stop in Miami." It is not a short poem, but worthy of fragmentary mention in our present book:

With Balseiro at the wheel, Land of Florida
Greetings, greetings, greetings,
Menéndez de Avilés. Full sail
To the gentleman of the hurricane wind!
What ever happened to Doña Antonia? Tell me of her,
Oh, flame of heated passions,
Hair flowing in the wind,
Unloved lover,
She stood sobbing, her body trembling,
Her voice rising above the pounding waves,
Breasts, high towers on a firm body,
But you, looking for Spanish towers,
Did not embark on her galleon?
Had I been second in command, my friend,
She would not have escaped me,
Though later I might have swung
From a high mast.
   Speed on, speed on,
   A woman, the sky, and the palms escape me.
Jasmine, blue sky and sounding sea,
See that woman with the golden hair,
With thighs of flowering desire,
Laughter on her lips, and soft warm breasts.
Give to Avilés the cross and somber decorum,
I prefer the fountains
Of eternal youth, whether a stream or a torrent,
The sun, the sea, the clear blue sky,
And the siren and the woman swimming.
   Speed on, speed on
   A woman, the sky, and the palms escape me.
Better than with Menéndez de Avilés, I'll go
With Ponce de León, who loved the bronzed sirens,
The feathered ring-doves.
Intoxicated with their perfume,
Instead of returning the maidens untouched,
He would undress them under the stars.
And even today, with foam of orange blossoms,
The waves of the seas sing a nuptial song
In the name of him who offered his ships

> To eyes as big as the morning star and to love.
>   Speed on, speed on.
>   A woman, the sky, and the palms escape me.
> Miami. Shore of foam. Fountains. Canals.
> No longer the Indian, his paddle and his canoe,
> Now, sirens of flesh and blood
> With arms for oars and a kiss on the lips,
> And a nakedness, a nakedness that has
> The shine and glow of marble.
> Into my memories the Spanish influence comes,
> And since all is confined to my illusion,
> When I see a copy of the Giralda
> My mind switches and the real Giralda appears
> With a cluster of gold, California carnations,
> Simulating flames.
> Gold of peaches gilded with honey,
> Gold in her faithful hands as in the branches.
>   Speed on, speed on,
>   A woman, the sky and the palms escape me.
> On Biscayne Avenue
> Tall helmeted palms,
> Green hair and slender shape.
> Palms and palms and more palms,
> Marching past in a throng,
> "What are you doing there Antillian palms?"
> And they reply gracefully, "We are
> Models for North American women,
> They borrow their eyes from the sea and the sky
> And from us our shape and height,
> Blond from the sun and short of hair;
> We give them their neck, voice and waist
> And in exchange for this grace,
> They give us the open spaces,
> The air and our roots, they give us all"
> In the canals are the ancient sails
> Beneath them are the doves, and above, the stars.
>   Speed on, speed on,
>   A woman, the sky and the palms escape me.
> All the Northern women are Amazons of red cheeks

All the Southern women have the sky in their eyes.
And if all this splender were not enough,
Brunettes from Puerto Rico, and sugar from Havana.

Thus, with historical references and Spanish gracefulness, Alfonso Camín has given us an impressionistic picture of Florida in days gone by and of Miami today.

As can be seen, the city was not lacking in intellectual acquaintances; although the ones previously mentioned, with the exception of Juan Ramón and Zenobia, were here only in passing.

Among the memories, Rómulo Gallegos and Andrés Eloy Blanco stand out. After a stay in Havana, they came to Star Island, one of the man-made islands between Miami and Miami Beach, as guests of a North American gentleman that had met them in Caracas. Gallegos, the famous Venezuelan novelist, had been recently ousted from the presidency of the Republic. His friend, Andrés Eloy Blanco, the splendid poet, had been his minister of foreign relations. Both men, each renowned as a literary figure of hemispheric stature, were overwhelmed by their political losses. It was pathetic to listen to Gallegos try to explain his downfall with an overabundance of reasons, as if he were still confused by the metamorphosis of events. I was gazing upon a helplessly saddened man. Fortunately, I had been forewarned by Ernesto de Aragón, a dear friend and well-known Havana doctor whom I had met through mutual relations, the Hernández-Catás. In his letter, Ernesto had asked me to visit Gallegos, who was at that moment in need of his friends. Andrés Eloy, reserved and subdued, always in command of his emotions, hardly said a word. Only when he spoke of poetry did his voice seem to forget his sadness.

When my family and I arrived in Florida, in 1946, invited by the president of the University of Miami to teach Hispanic literature, I found a nucleus of distinguished Hispanic-Americans in the community. Among my Puerto Rican countrymen, besides the factory workers and the farm hands, there were also medical doctors, dental surgeons, lawyers, industrialists, real estate men, agriculturists, bankers, and others. Among those interested in the cultural growth of the community was the family of Don Antonio Ferré, who had donated the graduate school building to the university. This same family would later give to politics the present mayor of the city of Miami, Maurice, after he had served in the Florida State Legislature.

General Introduction [17]

In the early fifties, a young Nicaraguan couple arrived from Panama to found a newspaper. Since then, *Diario Las Américas* has been the first with the most complete news about the Hispanic world. The newspaper is under the direction of Dr. Horacio Aguirre, one of the most listened-to voices of our community and of the Hispanic-American press.

Dr. Octavio Méndez Pereira, Aguirre's beloved professor and former president of the University of Panama, came to Miami on different occasions. Dr. Pereira and I, together with Colón Eloy Alfaro, attended the Caribbean Conferences at the University of Florida in Gainesville. Colón Eloy, the son of the great Ecuadorian president who was assassinated by his political opponents, had graduated from West Point and afterward came to Washington as the Ecuadorian ambassador. Later on, in his Panamanian home, I met Don Ricardo Alfaro, his relative and author of *Diccionario de anglicismos*.

North America, for multiple reasons, is historically obligated to Spain. Besides what has already been mentioned about Ponce de León and the extraordinary Pedro Menéndez de Avilés, territory that is now the United States was crossed and re-crossed by such men as Hernando de Soto and Cabeza de Vaca and Pánfilo de Narváez. They found the Mississippi, the prairies, the deserts, the high mountains, and stood on the shores of the Pacific. At about the same time the Pilgrims were landing, Santa Fe, the oldest city that is a state capital today, was founded in what is known as New Mexico. During the sixteenth, seventeenth, and eighteenth centuries the impact of the Spanish explorers and missionaries was felt from Florida to California. This truly incredible expansion was carried out by men of epic heroism and fortitude. Whoever is interested in those journeys, in which the explorations alternated between cruelty and charity, should read not only the chronicles of the Spaniards of that time, and modern Spanish historians, but also Charles F. Lummis' history about the sixteenth century. The book was translated and published in 1916 with a prologue by Don Rafael Altamira, who praises his outstanding North American colleagues for the honest and truthful way they present the Spanish discoverers and founders.

Although Ponce de León was unable to find the fabulous Fountain of Youth, García López de Cárdenas had the good fortune to discover the multicolored marvel of natural perfection that is the Grand Canyon in the territory of Arizona. Legends and magical reality interwove a tapestry of myth and truth, of illusion and solidity for those in search of the Promised Land. The wanderings of these adventurers crossed many latitudes. It was their efforts, added to the later contributions of other European countries, that identified the United States even before its birth as a remarkable example of transculturation. This is the basis of the importance of the so called "minority groups" to our national enrichment: an importance that, properly and wisely emphasized in 1976, will add to the prestige of the historical celebrations. Such a heritage should not be forgotten or destroyed. It commands our grateful reverence.

A good example of such attitude was demonstrated by Stanton Griffis, American ambassador to Spain, who upon arriving in New York on February 5, 1952, publicly recalled the Spanish monarch Charles III's loan to the Thirteen Colonies to buy uniforms, ammunition, and supplies for their fight against England. He justly made mention that for fifteen years Spain paid to Austria, Germany, Italy, and Holland the banking obligations that the colonies had been unable to honor. (Newspaper *Ya,* Madrid, February 6, 1952). Our ambassador's words were based on strict historical truth stated at the lecture of José Antonio Vaca de Osma, which dealt with the Spanish intervention during the American Revolution.[2] It is important to remember that at that moment, as well as on other occasions, Spain was acting in some respects contrary to her own best interests. When she favored the rebelling Thirteen Colonies, she indirectly invited her own ones in the Western Hemisphere to rebel. Spain was fighting the British in spite of the persisting rumor in Europe that Russia might provide England 20,000 men and some naval units to quench the American insurrection, a suggestion unacceptable to Catherine II. Although this anti-British action would eventually cost Spain her overseas empire, she stood firm by her decision to help the North American rebels.

Among the officers in the Spanish army that participated in the fight against the British for Pensacola in 1781 was a Venezuelan, Francisco de Miranda. In that important military engagement the American garrison had been rescued from the English by Bernardo de Gálvez, Spanish governor of Louisiana.[3] Miranda, born in Caracas on March 29, 1750, was already field officer of Gen. Juan Manuel Cagigal who, in February 1781 was governor of Cuba. It was during the first days of May of that same year that Miranda set foot on what would later be part of the United States. Because of his bravery in action, he was promoted to the rank of colonel. During his stay in Florida, he came to the conviction that the Spanish colonies to the south should follow the example of the thirteen northern

General Introduction [19]

colonies. And thus he wrote later on October 10, 1792: "and I thought it would be better to suffer for some time, and to wait patiently for the independence of the Anglo-American colonies, which would, in the future, lead without doubt to our own independence" (Miranda: Archives, vol. 8, p. 9). This is why Miranda is considered the forerunner of Spanish-American independence.

Dr. José Simón, a Cuban professor at Old Dominion University at Norfolk, Virginia, published on December 13, 1974, a documented article on the contribution of the "Havana Ladies" who, with the leadership of Cagigal and Miranda, helped the independence of the Thirteen Colonies. Dr. Simón based his work on Stephan Ronsal *(When The French Were Here: A Narrative of the Sojourn of the French Forces in America, and their Contribution to the Yorktown Campaign)* and on the American revolutionary correspondence (J. M. Jared Sparks, vol. 3). Simón reminds us, after describing the desperate economic situation of General Washington and his French allies, of the following:

> Saint-Simón finally arrived in Havana after a dangerous crossing due to the vigilance of the English fleet in the Caribbean. He immediately got into contact with the governor of the island, Juan Manuel Cagigal and his field-officer, Francisco Miranda.... Immediately, Miranda and other creoles formed a committee to collect funds for Saint-Simón. The financial contribution of the Havana business men, both Spaniards and creoles, was generous, but the principle group that made the collection effort possible was "the Havana Ladies." They offered their jewels and diamonds to the cause of liberty of this nation (the United States). According to ... the historian Charles Lee Lewis.... in his work about De Grasse, the amount of one million two hundred thousand pounds was placed aboard ship.[4]

If there were written documents, it would be appropriate to reproduce here the persuasive conclusions cited by the Puerto Rican historian, Aurelio Tió, to show that the first institution of general studies in the New World was to be established in San Juan, January 9, 1532, as approved by Pope Clement VII. (This information was in a letter written to me from Santurce, Puerto Rico, March 18, 1975, and had previously been published in the *Bulletin of the Puerto Rican Academy of History,* vol. 2, No. 5 (San Juan, Jan. 1, 1971), under the title of "The First University of America." (Dr. Ricardo E. Alegria, an anthropologist who is an authority on Puerto Rican culture, agrees with Tió's point of view, as expressed orally to the editor.)

England considered the conquest of Puerto Rico before and after the independence of the Thirteen Colonies. Dr. Arturo Morales Carrión, another most distinguished Puerto Rican historian, published in the *Caribbean Historical Review*s an essay entitled "Eighteenth Century Puerto Rico in Diplomacy and War," from which we quote:

> Before the outbreak of the American War of Independence, Puerto Rico continued to be a sore spot in the relations between England and Spain in the Middle West Indian area.... In 1753, Governor Ramírez de Estenós, upon hearing that English settlers from the Leeward Islands were establishing themselves on Vieques, organized an expedition with Spanish and Puerto Rican troops and fell upon the foreign colonists, destroying their plantations and taking them prisoners to San Juan. From that time on, it was customary for the Spanish authorities to send periodically reconnaisance parties to the neighboring islands to conduct a vigilant search for intruders.

Fourteen years after the victory of the Thirteen Colonies in 1797, and after Trinidad had surrendered to the British forces, two military figures, Adm. Henry Harvey and Gen. Sir Ralph Abercromby invaded Puerto Rico. They were soundly defeated thanks to the strong military fortifications and to the bravery of Capt. Gen. Don Ramón de Castro and the men under him. "Puerto Rico doesn't surrender. Puerto Rico has to be captured," he replied to the enemy.

With the recounting of acts such as these, we have tried to set up the antecedents and conduct of the Hispanic world which were so vital to the history of the rebel American colonies. The collaboration of France was of great importance. But it should not lead some European and United States historians, as has unfortunately happened from time to time, to value the French effort exclusively.[6] To quote one such lamentable example from a history book on the surrender of Cornwallis at Yorktown: "on October 19, 1781, the entire British army became prisoner of war. The French had at last rendered the service for which Franklin, in Paris, had pleaded so long and earnestly, and for which the American nation must forever be grateful." There is no mention of Spain's help: yet it was that same year, 1781, when the English garrison surrendered to the Spanish forces at Pensacola after a long and well-conducted battle.

Before Miranda had completed his independence plans for the South American countries, he was sent to Jamaica by the Spaniards to carry out a prisoner exchange. While there, he obtained military information on the island's fortifications for future reference. He returned to Cuba with some thousand Spanish soldiers. According to his detractors, he also brought back contraband goods for an English merchant. The cargo was supposedly unloaded at Batabanó.

General Introduction [21]

According to William S. Robertson, the well-informed American historian, the promotions granted to Miranda, and/or the favoritism bestowed on him by his superiors sparked jealousy and envy among certain Spanish officers. By royal command, his arrest was ordered. The warrant arrived while Miranda was away on a mission to New Providence in the Bahamas.[7]

Arrested in August 1782, he was soon freed by Governor Cagigal. The following year, he was condemned to ten years in prison, heavily fined, and lost his rank of colonel. But the sentence was so unjust that the Council of the Indies acquitted him of the charges, and acquitted Cagigal for having freed him. But Miranda had not waited around for the verdict. Believing that the Council would be prejudiced against him, he had fled Cuba with the intention of presenting his case personally before the king, Charles III. His route took him through the United States for the second time, landing in Newberne, North Carolina. After a year he traveled to Holland, the Crimea, Athens, and onto the banks of the Nova. In June 1789 he handed to William Pitt, then prime minister of Great Britain, a plan to promote the independence of Hispanic America. Unsuccessful in his attempt, he moved to France where he participated in the Revolution.

Miranda was a worldly man, favored by ladies amongst whom was Catherine II of Russia. She took him to Turkey and bestowed on him the rank of colonel in her army. In 1810, he returned to Venezuela. In December of that year, he inspired Venezuela's Declaration of Independence, but the struggle for independence was unsuccessful at that moment. In 1812, the Spanish commander, Domingo Monteverde, controlled the country. In La Guaira, betrayed to the new government, Miranda was arrested. He was taken to San Juan, Puerto Rico, where he remained incarcerated until he embarked for Spain. He died in prison in Cádiz, on July 14, 1816.

We have devoted adequate space to Miranda because he was a Hispanic-American who, while serving as an officer in the Spanish army, rebelled in an independence venture for his people. What is more, he had learned his lesson from the Thirteen Colonies. Lt. Gen. George Washington had also fought side by side with the British before he fought against them. Such would also be the case of General San Martín from Argentina. These three men, Washington, Miranda, and San Martín, were militarily molded by monarchical systems against which they eventually fought. Miranda, the universal Venezuelan, traveled through the lands of the early explorers: Spain, Cuba, Florida, Puerto Rico. He also visited a few North American cities, among them, Boston, New York, and Philadelphia. In Massachusetts, he met Lafayette who did not impress him favorably. In his journal, he wrote the following commentary: "He seems to be a mediocre personality, always in motion, full of activity like a *Galiciano*."[8] In spite of the orthographic and syntactical errors that fill his journal, there existed in Miranda a military and an intellectual curiosity that was far reaching. This desire for knowledge took him to West Point, Harvard, and Yale. While at these institutions, he visited the respective libraries and made careful note of the number of volumes in each. He remarked with astonishment on the fact that modern languages were not being taught.

Another important contribution made by Spain to the American revolutionary struggle was the capture of Natchez, Mississippi, by the previously named governor of Louisiana, Bernardo de Gálvez. An order from the Spanish overseas secretary (November 20, 1776) opened the port of Havana and the other colonial harbors to all rebel ships.

A year later, General Burgoyne surrendered in Saratoga. The news did not reach the American representative in Paris until the early days of December. Fate or chance once more intervened in the affairs of men, for the day the news arrived, Beaumarchais, the playwright, was dining with Benjamin Franklin. Beaumarchais, twice married to rich widows, was a generous friend to the cause of freedom. This man, author of *The Barber of Seville,* had organized a rather mysterious company to help raise funds for the North American colonies. The company, Rodríguez Hortalez et Cie., traded in military equipment for the colonies. Beaumarchais' activities were tolerated because of his friendship with the French ministers. Franklin, who had arrived in Paris a year before, had been unsuccessful, as had John Adams later, in convincing the French king to openly support the New World rebels. When the letter was read informing of Burgoyne's surrender, Beaumarchais, with Jefferson's prophetic words ringing in his ears—*"That these united colonies are, and of right ought to be, free and independent states,"* rushed to Versailles. Unfortunately in his hurry, the coach overturned and Beaumarchais was injured. Nevertheless, the communication reached Louis XVI who *then* authorized favorable commercial treaties and an alliance with the Colonies (February 6, 1778).

John Hay, plenipotentiary minister in Madrid, was not as successful, for he had to contend with the "absurd meticulosity of the Spanish court,"[9] to which the surrender of Burgoyne was meaningless. The moment passed and nothing was accomplished. This in spite of Franklin's vigorous

General Introduction [23]

backing of Spain in its contention with England over Gibraltar. Despite the important help rendered by Spain to the Thirteen Colonies, Spain did not benefit from the war against England. Little or nothing is known by Americans in general of her important participation in the aid for the independence of the first republic of the New World.

The new nation was on its way. Yet independence and liberty are not necessarily the same thing. The first years after independence had been won did not bring about effective government. The Articles of Confederation were useless papers for the national government. A constitution was needed. In a letter of 1784, Jefferson warned James Madison, "I find the conviction growing strongly that nothing can preserve our confederacy unless the bond of union, their common council, be strengthened." Washington, two years later, would confirm Jefferson's warning, "I do not conceive that we can exist long as a nation without having lodged somewhere a power which will pervade the whole union in as energetic a manner as the authority of the state government extends over the several states."

Delegates named by governors or state legislatures were authorized to convoke an assembly to amend the Articles of Confederation. It was apparently with this purpose that they met in Philadelphia on May 20, 1787. At that meeting, which would last four months, there were some among the fifty-five initial members that were thinking of their own best interests. There was, however, an intellectual minority of extremely capable delegates who would undertake the promotion and authorization of the longest-lasting governing articles. Although Jefferson was absent (for he was serving as plenipotentiary minister to France), Franklin, the noble patriarch of quick wit and subtle humor, was there. Franklin and Jefferson were probably the two most cultured North Americans of their time. If Jefferson excelled in idealism, gifted graphic expression, and political ability, Franklin excelled in his scientific discoveries and pragmatic and persuasive character: he was a man of the world. And they were both always ready to serve their country in its hour of crisis and need.

Amidst a torrent of passionate arguments and inflammatory speeches, Alexander Hamilton, the islander of acute intelligence (born in Nevis, British West Indies), became the aristocratic model of good speech and of judicious, although at times stubborn Federalist thought. Quite different physically, was Madison, the 36-year-old Virginian. He possessed uncanny judicial intuition and was exceptionally knowledgeable in law.

Washington presided over the assembly, an austere presence, still in uniform, so as to remind all of his military victories and of his country's debt to him.

One of the political sins of the Constitution is not an original sin. It did not abolish slavery, but neither had Greece, the birth place of democracy, and the great republic of Brazil did not free its slaves until 1888, although there it was accomplished peacefully. (But a comparison would not be valid at this time.) A young Jefferson, when he joined the Virginia House of Burgesses (1769) proposed the abolition of slavery, although he was himself a slave owner. He was unsuccessful. Also during colonial days, Franklin had organized an anti-slavery society. Why wasn't the idea established at the Constitutional Assembly in Philadelphia? Because there were some among the delegates who fought the issue bitterly and would have hindered the approval of the Constitution. To its proponents, it was of greater urgency to begin with the functional principles of the republic. ("First things first," insisted a cautious Franklin).

At the moment of signing the Constitution, of the fifty-five original delegates there remained only thirty-nine. And the task of its ratification by the thirteen states was still ahead. However, our present republican form of government, which has lasted the longest, politically, of any nation in the world, was established. It has lasted due to the willingness to compromise that exists in this country. And, as Washington had forseen, it prepared an open road for future amendments which would revitalize, as needed, the original document.

Every rule has an exception and the tragic Civil War was ours. But, then too, the Union was saved. Another colossal figure at that time was able to preserve national authority over segregational fever.

Originally Franklin had advanced the symbolic notion that the colonies were like clocks that had been set "to make thirteen clocks strike as one." Later Daniel Webster in his memorable debate with Hayne would coin the phrase, "Liberty *and* Union, now and forever, one and inseparable." Much later, Lincoln would accept war as the last resource to save the Union, honoring the motto of *E Pluribus Unum*.[9]

In this land, from Florida (the first explored) to California, Spain left its ineffaceable print. The new country's founders were capable of developing a political constitution—a true revolutionary political system—for which they were praised all over the world. The British statesman William Gladstone said, "It is the greatest work ever *struck off* at any time by the mind and purpose of man." (Italics are ours.) Could those words perhaps

General Introduction [25]

suggest that the Constitution was merely a chance occurrence? The truth is that its light did not shine instantly. It was the result of judicious, liberal, long, profound, and at times, violent disputes and painful deliberations. The investigations of R. L. Schuyler prove that the essential agreements prevailed in the long run. Although figures such as Patrick Henry, Samuel Adams, Jefferson, and Paine were absent, the statesmen won the battle against the politicians. Washington, whose moral authority was at all times so valuable, said, "It was for a long time doubtful whether we were to survive as an independent republic, or decline from our federal dignity into insignificant and withered fragments of empire."

Let us take a quick glance at the reaction of some of the Hispanic-American founders:

In 1810, in his *Plan of General Defense for All America,* Don Juan Egaña (born in Lima, and one of the outstanding figures in civil life in Chile, the birthplace of his father) advocated a confederacy of states in our hemisphere. He added that the chief of the confederacy would have to be the nation which was the founder of the republican system on the Continent and that Washington should be the capital since it was the capital of "the first nation to set the example of freeing itself from tyranny and despotism."

In 1813, the instructions given by José Artigas, liberator of Uruguay, to the official delegates to the Constitutional Assembly meeting in Buenos Aires were based on the United States model.

On September 6, 1815, in his letter from Jamaica, Bolívar praised "the talent and political virtues that characterize our brothers from the North." The Liberator emphasized this idea four years later at the Congress of Angostura.

In 1823, the greatest of the Hispanic-American humanists, Andrés Bello, advocated the independence of the New World but not only from a political viewpoint. In spite of his many years in England, in spite of his classical formation, the Venezuelan educator was also interested in the cultural independence of our continent. The idea was not new. In 1783, Noah Webster, the famous lexicographer, had anticipated Bello when he proclaimed, "America must be as independent in literature as in politics." Interestingly enough, there is no proof of whether Bello knew of Webster's statement.

Federalism triumphed in Mexico. On October 1824, a new Constitution was proclaimed which mirrored that of the United States with two exceptions: (1) all prior privileges and exemptions were to continue, and (2) there would be no trial by jury.

When, in the following year, the Ecuadorian José Joaquín Olmedo praised Bolívar in his "Song to the Victory of Junín," he alludes to the United States with gratitude. He almost deifies Washington:

> And those happy people
> Freer than all others
> Are praised for their glory and power.
> Among the stars,
> The star of Virginia shines.
> It brings us the blessed kiss
> Of fraternal friendship.

Much would have to be said about Faustino Domingo Sarmiento, the Argentinian patriarch who so well loved and admired the United States. Perhaps it suffices to quote from him "Let us not stop the United States in its march as many propose. Let us catch up with the United States. Let us form one America as all the waters of the seas become one ocean, let us all be one United States."

In her sonnet "To Washington" (1841), the Cuban poetess Gertrudis Gómez de Avellaneda praises the man she considers superior to Napoleon.

> The past had no model for your virtue,
> Nor will history provide a copy for the future,
> Nor will anyone else equal the greatness of your memory
> Which the centuries will sing of in their flight.

> Europe saw its land bloodied
> By the genius of war and victory,
> But it was America to which
> Heaven granted the genius of good.

> May the daring conqueror enjoy his triumph
> While he turns the earth into a wasteland,
> May his vanity be served by all the slaves at his command.

> But people know well in their hearts
> That only he who makes them free is strong
> That only he who makes them great is great!

Testimonies such as these, because of their good will, seemed to predict future friendship among the nations of America. Nevertheless, four years later, "those first joyous people" would declare war on Mexico. It was such an unjust and unpopular war that the United States failed in its recruitment of volunteers. This act of aggression was denounced by many great Americans. The list of these illustrious men gives evidence of the moral fiber that characterizes this nation even at its darkest moments. Writers, legislators, and even first-ranking military leaders condemned the unfairness of the act. Emerson, Thoreau, Lincoln, John Quincy Adams, Daniel Webster, Henry Clay, Calhoun, Robert E. Lee, and U. S. Grant were among those that expressed themselves against the politics of President Polk, who had provoked such an unconstitutional and unnecessary war.

Would it be easy to find in other countries a similar representation of ethical values? It is fitting to remember that along side these dark waters of indifference, arrogance, deafness, blunders, short-sightedness, and political failure we can hear in the national life stream the protest of the civic-minded citizenry that judiciously triumphs over public corruption.

But let us return to the nineteenth century and the examples of friendship toward the United States and the recognition of the importance of its example for the other countries.

Miguel de Unamuno said, speaking of Juan Montalvo, that untiring prosecutor of the oppressors of his country (Ecuador), "He triumphed over tyranny, not because he imitated Cervantes but because he imitated Don Quixote."[10] In effect, his pen seemed afire. Whether in his native land or in exile, he did not cease his attack against the despots. In 1875, he brought about the presidential downfall of García Moreno, the dictator who was assassinated by one of Montalvo's disciples. He was equally harsh on Moreno's successor, Ignacio Veintimilla. To emphasize his beliefs, in 1882 Montalvo wrote in the *Siete Tratados (Seven Treaties)* immemorable pages about Washington and Bolívar. He admitted, subtly, that the United States had had from its beginning the service of men dedicated to freedom:

> and if the leader had been killed, one hundred Washingtons would have stepped forward to fill the vacuum, and they would have done the job well. Washington was surrounded by men as noble as he and as dedicated: Jefferson, Madison, men of deep thoughts; Franklin, the genius of land and sky who not only wrests the sceptre from the hands of tyrants, but seized the lightning from the skies... .

Martí lived in the United States for about fourteen years. No

Hispanic-American wrote as much about this nation. The pages in his *North American Scenes* occupy fourteen volumes and his collection, *The Americans*, fills three volumes. Among these essays, there is one commenting on the twenty-eighth of September 1887, in which he writes about the Constitution of Philadelphia, calling it "a noble government machine." He points out that if there were indeed three major areas of differences among the delegates, there were also three compromises. "Unable to defeat each other, they would set aside differences in favor of vital mutual interests." The rule of "virtuous politics" prevailed, for "it is the only durable and useful solution."

This was the image that the Constitution had cast upon the world. It had not been enough to delight in "a useless national pride." It had been necessary to determine "by law that the union was indispensable to the existence of the nation." Remembering that glorious agreement of 1787 where the interests of all had been reconciled, Martí wrote that "never was liberty so real," and that mankind, as never before, had taken a firm step into the future. Later on, Martí refers to the United States as "the best house of liberty." Tributes, such as these, appear repeatedly in his work.

But when moved by his interest in inter-American politics, or suspicious that his homeland could become a victim to the power of the United States, Martí ceases being a man of all ages and all countries. Under such circumstances, the memory of imperialistic efforts are more vivid than the idea of this country, "as the only free homeland in the Universe" for all mankind.

He feared that the Antilles would become a stepping stone for the United States to move into South America. Thus, he exclaims, "I know the monster well, for I have lived in its entrails."

The American nationalists are offended by Martí's words. The enemies of the United States make malicious use of them to attack this country. Both seem to forget the painful occasion in which they were written. The words are an explosion of a hyperesthetic Martí overwhelmed by the loss to the Cuban revolution of three ammunition ships which had been confiscated by the American government. Jorge Mañach describes Martí's condition: his strenuous travels had produced an "inguinal infarct" which kept him immobilized." Martí was under an unrelenting pressure which, as Félix Lizaso has well said, "was constant during the last years of his restless life."

In a reminiscence by Emilio Pacheco (San José de Costa Rica, July

General Introduction [29]

1893), the following scene at the law school was described: "We saw Martí enter the hall, pale and slightly bent down, leaning on the arm of his friend Dr. Zambrana, until he reached the chair that had been reserved for him. Martí was a sick man."

Today, Cuba having set aside Martí's profound teachings, hundreds of thousands of his countrymen have found a new home for themselves in the United States; and particularly in Florida; and specially in Metropolitan Miami.

Almost two centuries after the Declaration of Independence and the Constitutional Assembly in Philadelphia, we remind ourselves of certain facts:

(1) That the Civil War having ended, Abraham Lincoln was unable to repeat Washington's words when signing the Constitution, "I did not think it possible to have come thus far without bloodshed."

(2) That more than once, the nation which rose from such noble premises has deviated from its initial intention. As any other human enterprise "the best house of liberty" has not always been administered by men as well intentioned as the founding fathers.

(3) That it is time for us to overcome the superiority complex which has motivated the actions of so many "ugly Americans," just as our detractors should overcome their unhealthy prejudice against us. In spite of some comparisons to the contrary, Caliban is not the archetype for the United States. Rubén Darío thought this at first, but his honesty and intellectual maturity, his studies and observations, his comparisons and experience led the universally famous Hispanic-American poet to rectify his opinion.[11]

(4) That we should study the history of the United States so that we might learn, as others have, of the economic help Spain gave to the Thirteen Colonies since the beginning of hostilities with England. Later Spain went as far as to declare war on England (1779).

(5) That Jefferson, the wise man from Monticello, having just freed English America from the mother country should refer to the nations to the south as Spanish America, not as Latin America. He, who, like Franklin, knew so well the culture of France and who loved so dearly the landscape of Italy, wrote, "Spanish America is all in revolt."[12]

(6) That we should surmount petty nationalism. Let us remember that during Washington's presidency and later during the war of 1812, two

secretaries of the Treasury, Alexander Hamilton and Albert Gallatin, were not native Americans. What is more, of the fifty-five signers of the Constitution, nine had been born abroad.

(7) That in the first session of the House of Burgesses in colonial Virginia, young Jefferson presented a motion which remained unheard, to free all slaves.

(8) That voting in public elections, more than a right slightly used, is a duty in which we all must share.

(9) That we should praise the fact that in the creation of the Constitution, there were men of the intellectual stature of the octogenerian Franklin as well as the twenty-two-year-old Rufus King, a determined anti-slavery delegate.

(10) That we should not forget that upon this soil, a man not of the white race was the first to give his life to the cause of liberty. (Was he a Natick Indian?) The fact also stands out that in an *official* report of 1778, there were about fifty-four black men in each of Washington's battalions.

(11) That in the sixteenth century, a dark-skinned African, named Estebanillo by the Spaniards, arrived in Florida with an expedition led by Alvar Núñez Cabeza de Vaca. Estebanillo explored Tampa Bay, Tallahassee, and Pensacola. He crossed this land from east to west. He went into Mexican territory and traveled through what is today Arizona, New Mexico, and Texas. The "Cibola" Indian women felt strongly attracted to this stranger, and some jealous husbands assassinated him during one of his scouting trips for the expedition of Fr. Marcos de Niza. Even before Estebanillo's journeys, in an account of early Florida exploration, the name of Jorge, a black seaman, appears. This same name reappears among the list of the eight cabin boys who came in Ponce de León's first expedition (perhaps a careless repetition?).

(12) That we should maintain eternal vigilance on our national interests and its administrators. Let us avoid being trapped by those who, singing Lorelei's songs, wish to expand their political doctrines. Let not disinterest nor innocence allow unscrupulous leaders free reign to commit our country to hidden enemies.

Only enlightened men in North, South, and Central America, freeing themselves of arbitrary and unjust mental burdens, can appreciate the extraordinary scientific and artistic contributions that the United States has made. Let us not continue any further; there are those blinded either by ignorance or by malice who can not see the truth.

General Introduction

Let no country consider itself fundamentally superior to its neighbor, or overestimate its own strength.

So that all our hemisphere may someday fulfill Bolívar's dream and be a Continent of Hope, we must begin with a reciprocal reexamination of our collective conscience. Mental hygiene is needed on all sides in order to amend errors and avoid surprises. The best humanitarian and civic program can be summarized in the words of one of the greatest presidents of the United States, Harry S. Truman: "We want to...do things in peace that we have been unable to do in war. If we can put this tremendous machine of ours...to work for peace, we can look forward to the greatest age in the history of mankind." That should be the goal of the United States as it approaches the twenty-first century. There should be a complete rededication to the ideals of the immortal Thomas Paine who, although born in England, when he came to Philadelphia became such a forceful voice for the freedom of the Thirteen Colonies: "The sun never shined on a cause of greater worth."

In closing, I wish to express once more my gratitude to the mayor of Miami, and to Metropolitan Dade County. I am thankful to Aida Deymier for her willingness to help us in our undertaking. I could not close these remarks without mentioning Mrs. Joseph Freeman and William Robertson who have done some of the proofreading.

The exemplary diligence of my wife, Mercedes, was of unforgettable value to me in my task. I thank all of the participants in making this work possible. Finally, I would like to recognize my debt to the National Endowment for the Humanities in Washington, D.C., and to state that the points of view here expressed are not necessarily those of the foundation.

NOTES

[1] *See* José Agustín Balseiro, *Expresión* de Hispanoamérica, vol. 1, 2nd ed. (Madrid; Gredos, 1970), pp. 247-261.

[2] This lecture was delivered at the International Program for Foreigners at the Maricel Palace in Sitges, Spain, July 21, 1951.

[3] Galveston, the Texas city, was named for Gálvez.

[4] José Simon, "The Cubans Saved George Washington" (Miami, Dec. 13, 1974). As I tried to prove, this was not the only gesture. Some examples have been mentioned previously, and others will be cited later, which give evidence to a series of Hispanic contributions to the victory of the Thirteen Colonies. Indeed, the most generous donation of the "Havana Ladies," when Washington and Rochambeau's chests were almost empty, was important in bringing about the final victory over Cornwallis.

[5] Vol. 1 (Dec. 1950), p. 4, The facts concerning the abortive invasion of 1797 may be found in the works of Dr. Morales Carrión, *History of the Puerto Rican People: From their Origin to the XVIII Century* (San Juan: Editorial de Instrucción Pública, 1968), chap. 21.

[6] Recall, for example, the struggle that the young and impetuous Marquis de Lafayette had in order to get the French monarch's permission to come to the colonies. He had to depart from Spain (at Los Pasajes, close to San Sebastián) for America.

[7] Francisco de Miranda, *The Diary of Francisco de Miranda: Tour of the United States, 1783-1784* (New York, 1928), intro., p. xv.

[8] Miranda, Diary, p. 121.

[9] Vaca de Osma, lecture (July 21, 1951), p. 29.

[10] One of Montalvo's most ambitious works is entitled *The Chapters that Cervantes Forgot.*

[11] See our two chapters discussing this subject in *The Americas Look at Each Other* (Coral Gables, Fla.: University of Miami Press, 1969), pp. 59-80.

[12] Bernardo Mayo, *Jefferson Himself: The Personal Narrative of a Many-Sided American* (Boston: Houghton Mifflin Co., 1942), Chap. 15.

"FLORIDA"
So named by Juan Ponce de León, the first to name the lands and rivers of the northern continent in the New World
by Vicente Murga*

Proposed Agreement

In his *General History of Spanish Activities in the Islands and Continents of the New World,* Antonio de Herrera described Ponce de León's departure as, "Juan Ponce de León departed, northerly bound, from the island of San Juan [later called Puerto Rico; the capital city continued to be called San Juan] on March 3." According to Garcilaso de la Vega, "the Inca," Ponce de León sighted land on the twenty-seventh of March 1513, and gave it the name of Florida, having arrived on Easter Sunday. Fr. Jerónimo de Oré states that this solemn holy day was often called by the Spaniards, *"Pascua Florida"* ("Flowered Paschal"). Many examples of the use of this name are found in legal documents of the time.

Having reviewed all the material published on this subject up to September 1974, I gave careful thought to the title of this chapter. I would like to suggest that all historians and geographers interested in this theme come to a consensus on the reliability of our sources so that the editors of encyclopedias, biographies, dictionaries, and textbooks may have available clear, undisputable, basic information.

With this in mind, let us begin.

The Voyage

The trip took place in 1513. In the original document from the office of naval registry, there is a statement on the departure of an expedition on

---
*Translated by Piedad F. Robertson.

January 29, 1513, from the Port of Yuma, Salvaleón township, province of Higüey, in the island of Española or Hispaniola (today Santo Domingo) to search for the island of Bimini and other lands. The expedition sailed to the port of Puerto Rico or San Germán and from there on March 3 to the discovery of the new lands. (Photocopy of the document may be found in my book *Juan Ponce de León* [San Juan: Editorial Universitaria, University of Puerto Rico, 1959].)

That the discovery was indeed made in 1513—instead of 1512 as is sometimes claimed—can be clearly established by an examination of the Church calendar. At first glance the difference of a year—1512 or 1513—does not seem as important as the name given to the new land. Yet, one should remember that the celebration of this religious festival and consequently all the dates of the itinerary would vary from year to year, since Easter is linked to the Jewish Passover which is celebrated in the Nisan full-moon cycle.

In the early days, there were differences between the Roman Church and the Asian Church. In Rome, Easter Sunday was celebrated the Sunday following the fourteenth of Nisan. The Asian Church celebrated it on the fourteenth of Nisan. The Nicean Concilium—in the year 325—settled this difference and set the date for Easter Sunday on the Sunday that follows the full moon after the spring equinox (March 21). As a result, the celebration of Easter may fall on any date between March 22 and April 25.

In the year 1513, Easter Sunday was on March 27 and in the year 1512 it was on April 11.

"The Inca" in his history, *Florida*, written in 1592 and published in Lisbon in 1605 after being reviewed and approved by Herrera in his position as official chronicler, has the following statement: "The first Spaniard to discover Florida was Juan Ponce de León. Since it was on Easter Sunday when he first sighted land, he named it Florida. This was in the year 1513, and the Church enumerators state that Easter that year was on the seventeenth of March."

In a notarized document given in Seville on the tenth of March 1508, to Doña Francisca Ponce de León, cousin of Juan Ponce de León, it is stated that the ship *San Telmo* was chartered to carry merchandise to the Indies and to be ready to load the supplies in twenty days from the date on the document and as late as eight days after Flowered Paschal (Easter Sunday) of that year.

"*Florida*"

This information should suffice to prove that the term Flowered Paschal instead of Easter Sunday was acceptable usage in documents and was a generalized idiom amongst the people in the days of Ponce de León.

The Successful Voyage Either in 1512 or 1513 Changes the Life of Juan Ponce de León

In the lawsuit of May 5, 1511, between the Spanish Crown and Admiral Don Diego Colón (Columbus) about the government and administration of justice in the name of the king of Castille on the island of Hispaniola as well as other islands discovered by Christopher Columbus (his father), the king, Don Fernando, handed down on May thirty-first the decision ordering Ponce de León to restore the staff of office of head constable of the island of San Juan to Miguel Díaz to hold and use in the name of Admiral Colón. He also ordered on June 6, 1511, the restoration of the mayor's staff of the island of San Juan to Juan Cerón. In a letter dated July 21, 1511, he added, "As for you, see in which way you may best serve us over there and write to me about it, or leaving someone to supervise your property there, come to see me so as to inform me of affairs over there and what you may wish to undertake so that I may make arrangements to help in whichever way I can."

When Ponce de León had been appointed captain governor of the island of San Juan on March 2, 1510, he had requested that Juan Cerón and Migual Díaz turn over to him the authority they had been exercising. When they refused, Ponce de León, making use of the power granted him by the king, had arrested them and Cerón's lieutenant, Diego de Morales, and sent them all back to Castille in a ship captained by Juan Bono de Quejo. This is why the royal decree said "restore" authority, and in the instructions given by Don Fernando to Cerón and Miguel Díaz on July 25, 1511, it is stated, "First, that after you arrive at said island you will take charge as I have ordered of your respective positions. Do this with good form so that you will not arouse anger and no one may think that you bear animosity toward Juan Ponce de León for what happened amongst you. Because if the islanders, especially those who have served Juan Ponce, notice such an attitude there would be great unrest which would be a disservice to the Crown. That is why it is convenient that you treat Juan Ponce, his friends and relations well so that they may become your followers and that affairs in the island may settle down."

Cerón, Díaz, and Morales arrived at the island towards the end of October or the beginning of November 1511. Possibly in the same ship or in another, a few days later, Francisco de Lizaur came also. He had been appointed accountant to the island of San Juan on April 15, by royal decree and confirmed on May 2, 1511. His arrival was carefully timed to be after Ponce de León stepped down as governor of the island and Don Diego took over. In this conscious delay one can find, perhaps, a clue to Lizaur's "turncoat" life.

Lizaur had first come to the island of Hispaniola with Ovando in 1502; he acted as his secretary and returned with Ovando to Castille after the arrival of Don Diego Colón (July 10, 1509) to govern the island by royal decree until the pending court case had been settled.

The close ties between Lizaur and Ovando and the friendship of Ovando and Juan Ponce de León, all of which Bartolomé de las Casas was witness to for many years, served to make believable the malicious stories about Ponce de León, invented by some "anonymous" source and related to las Casas. The credulity and good faith of las Casas is surprising. He made careful note of all the information his source provided him and later transmitted it to the regent of the kingdom of Castille, Cardenal Cisneros, and to the tribunal of history.

Cerón and Miguel Díaz de Aux wrote on November 28, 1511, of the terrible and fraudulent administration of the royal lands by Ponce de León and of the exploitation of the mines and the labor companies which were in violation of the agreement between Ovando, in the King's name, and Ponce de León. For this reason, Don Diego Colón arrived at the island and ordered on November 19, 1511, a special and unexpected melting of gold. Don Fernando wrote in response on February 23, 1512, that he was "deeply troubled" by this need. Cerón and Díaz further stated that they had found the Indians in a state of revolt, that pacification had not been attempted nor was any negotiator available, and that fighting continued with the local Indians and the Caribs.

The strategy they employed to bring about the destruction of a good and loyal servant, a man of great qualities was sly, bold, intelligently planned, and successful. They knew the King would demand proofs of their statements. Therefore, they would need an intermediary. They found him in the first royal accountant residing on the island of San Juan, Francisco de Lizaur, who with other royal officials was in charge of the royal lands, and who in a brief and damaging statement on November 30,

"Florida"

1511, to Don Fernando confirmed Ponce de León's mismanagement of the royal lands.

Events of the Year 1512

In the town of Puerto Rico on the island of San Juan, on January 20, 1512, in the presence of the mayor, Juan Cerón, the lieutenant accountant, García Troche, handed over all the books and documents in his power to Francisco de Lizaur, the chief accountant. They now had in their hands all the means necessary to distort information.

Don Fernando, foreseeing this maneuver, tried to cut them short in a letter dated February 23, 1512: "Of what you tell me on how peacefully and well received you were does not surprise me for I would not expect differently from Juan Ponce."

"I am very surprised at the ill state of affairs in which you have found the royal lands under Juan Ponce for I think highly of his ability. If you have not asked him to render an account of the situation yet, do not do so. But take into consideration the present state of affairs at the moment you receive this letter for I will ask for a complete statement." On that same day he appointed Sancho Velázquez to make an inventory of the royal lands, comparing it to the previous inventory prepared by the Prefect Father Nicolás Ovando with Ponce de León. He ordered Velázquez by royal decree to investigate the responsibility incurred by Ponce de León in such matters and to act justly and with care. Sancho Velázquez arrived in October and we will now follow closely all his actions.

Before arriving at the island he wrote the following instructions (September 9, 1511) to Cerón and Díaz with regard to the placement of the Indians: "I had ordered Juan Ponce to carry out the placement of the Indians on the island as he saw fit…he did this and has sent me a copy of the distribution which I am enclosing … therefore, I order you not to change in any way what he has done because as you well know the distribution and placement of the Indians is not within the jurisdiction of the Admiral."

On the same day, Velázquez also wrote to Don Diego Colón informing him of his letter to Cerón and Miguel Díaz about the placement of the Indians and ordering him not to interfere. "I have repeatedly told them in my letters that they should come to some agreement with Juan Ponce and that in no way should they hold anything that has transpired against him or any of his followers. They should not show any hatred towards them or ill-treat them in any way."

In spite of the insistent handwritten decrees, shortly after their arrival, Cerón and Miguel Díaz interfered and carried out a new distribution of the Indians. The king, Don Fernando, upon being notified of their actions wrote to them, "The information which you sent with regard to the Indians and other persons on the island seems to be justified and in accordance with your responsibilities, and seems to have been carried out without causing any hatred or ill feeling, looking only for the best way to serve us, for the good of the island, for the proper treatment and conservation of the Indians. Since I believe that you have told me the truth, I hope that when I order an investigation on such matters I do not discover contradictory information, for you would then be in a difficult position. The truth can never be hidden."

In that same letter of February 23, 1512, he told them, "You should try not to change things too much for you know how hard it is on the Indians to be moved from one place to another, and this is bad for our affairs... once more I order you to carefully look into these affairs."

Cerón and Miguel Díaz, with the approval of Don Diego Colón, took the Indian workers from Iñigo de Zúñiga, and gave them to Alonso de Cea, in violation of the distribution made by Ponce de León. They also took the Indian workers from Pedro de Cárdenas. Juan Bono de Quejo was imprisoned in spite of Don Fernando's letter (January 31, 1511) to Don Diego, as punishment for having been the captain of the ship which had taken Cerón and Miguel Díaz in detention back to Spain. This was a serious offense for it overruled Bono de Quejo's privilege as a nobleman who could not be arrested like a commoner.

To add to all this, Ponce de León was unable to leave the island. Cerón and Miguel Díaz, with the backing of the council of the town of Puerto Rico, by claiming an emergency confiscated the ship that Ponce de León had bought from Gil Romero. At this moment, the accountant Lizaur interceded and offered to get Juan Ponce a caravel if he would advance Lizaur 1,000 *castellanos*. This was done, but in the end Ponce de León was left without the caravel or the money.

The accountant Lizaur, with the books and documents in his power, then asked the lieutenant governor, Francisco de Cardona, for an accounting of the money due the King from the sale of slaves captured during the recent Indian war. The King's share in such transactions was always twenty percent of the sale price. The battles had been fought by the forces of Ponce de León as a result of an Indian attack on the settlement of Aguada in which Don Cristóbal de Sotomayor, son of the Count of Camiña, and his nephew, Don Diego, and five other Christians had been killed and the village burned. Many other Spaniards who were working in the mines nearby were wounded in the action.

These events took place towards the end of 1510 or the beginning of 1511 while Juan Ponce was governor of the island and Don Cristóbal de Sotomayor was head constable in replacement of Miguel Díaz, who had been sent as a prisoner back to Castille.

Don Cristóbal de Sotomayor had been secretary to Queen Germana, the young wife of King Fernando. When he decided to leave for the island of San Juan on January 9, 1509, he was granted royal permission to establish himself and all of his followers in whichever part of the island of San Juan that most pleased him. On the day of his departure, the King wrote a letter recommending Sotomayor to Admiral Don Diego, and to the governor of the island of San Juan ordering them to give to Don Cristóbal, and to those in his company, lands, property, and an allotment of Indian servants. Sotomayor and his companions departed in May 1509, and arrived at the island of Hispaniola on July 5, 1509. There they waited for the arrival of Don Diego who immediately assigned to them Agüeybana, a principal Indian chief, and all of the chiefs under him. Agüeybana was the Indian chief who had previously welcomed and entertained Ponce de León when he first arrived on August 12, 1508.

Marcos de Aguilar informs us that Agüeybana was related to the Indian chief, Andrés, from the province of Higüey. This should give us a clue to better understand the warm reception Agüeybana gave Ponce de León and the behavior of the latter when he heard of the deaths of Sotomayor and his party, the absence of reprisals; and the moderation in the wars or confrontations with the rebelling Indian chiefs. In respect to the truth, it should be here stated that there is no original document, or a copy of one, with an official account of these confrontations sent to Don Fernando by Ponce de León. All that is known today is in royal letters from the King commenting on the events.

Lizaur also gave us revealing information when he looked into affairs to determine if Ponce de León had paid Don Fernando the customary one-fifth of the profits from the sale of slaves taken during the Indian encounters. Only once did Captain Governor Ponce de León, accompanied by Spaniards and Indians in his service, directly take part in these campaigns. In that encounter he took sixty-eight slaves, including children and women. They were auctioned publicly and the treasurer wrote down the King's fifth share from each sale, plus the name of the person who had acquired the Indian slave, man, woman, or child. Ponce de León sold two slave women and paid the tribute of two *pesos* for one and three *pesos* for the other (all of which is in the original documents, published in my work). At that same time mention is made of Capt. García Cansyno who had laid siege to a village and captured nine slaves, including women and children, who were auctioned off like the others.

Ponce de León then requested the subordinate Indian chiefs to surrender peacefully without fear of reprisals. The word "request" is included in the documents, a fact which caused amusement for it had never before been thus used in official proceedings. Ponce de León's request was the slightest form of admonition. The Indians that served him were living testimony to all that peaceful coexistence was possible and beneficial to both parties. It so happened, however, that not all listened to his admonitions, and the chieftains who had not submitted then confronted Capt. Sancho de Arango, Captain Salazar and Capt. Luis de Añasco. Sancho de Arango captured twenty-eight slaves. Salazar captured twenty, and Luis de Añasco brought back two. An auction sale and tribute payment were completed as before.

On September 28, 1514, Ponce de León, upon request from Pedro Sotomayor, the son of Don Cristóbal, declared in the town of Valladolid, before Gil González de Avila, chancellor in the royal court of the Queen, "That I know that when Don Cristóbal died he owned an Indian chief called Agüeybana and that he had many other Indians, but the exact number is not known. That these were given to him by the Admiral. That the chief together with his captains and other subordinate chiefs had about six hundred subjects. That after the death of Don Cristóbal, I as well as others were witness to the distribution of the Indians and do so state it." He distributed the Indians; he did not kill them.

Don Fernando approved of the tactics used by Ponce de León, and in a letter dated September 9, 1511, he recommended that Cerón and Miguel Díaz do likewise. "Ponce de León wrote to me of how he had twice requested the island chiefs who had rebelled to surrender to him and how in my name all their crimes would be forgiven. He informed me of all the measures he took to try to convince them, but was able only to win over two of the captains. He then defeated the other rebelling Indians and in order to avoid a slaughter of the Indians by the Christians, he allowed all who participated in controlling the rebellion to take the Indian captives as

"*Florida*"

slaves. I think that he acted well. You will do the same, for otherwise there would be a slaughter of Indians. You should further see to it that those who have Indian slaves treat them well."

Cerón and Miguel Díaz, instead of following the example of Ponce de León and obeying the orders of the King, established in the first days of March, 1512, *entradas* or *cabalgadas* (hunting parties) to hunt down the Indians in their lands for the sole purpose of capturing Indians to be sold into slavery and so enrich the Treasury. And it is so stated in the Treasury books.

Ponce de León was able to send Iñigo de Zúñiga to Castille to inform the King of the tragic happenings on the island of San Juan and of his own confinement which kept him from personally reporting to the King. Meanwhile, Ponce waited patiently for the arrival of Sancho de Velázquez.

The first act of the King was to discharge Francisco de Lizaur, the accountant, and have him returned to Castille as a prisoner.

Sancho de Velázquez arrived at the island of San Juan in the first days of October 1512. He began his work by requesting immediately a clear accounting of Ponce's business for the King. According to the first agreement of June 1508, between Ponce de León and the general plenipotentiary governor of the Indies, Fr. Nicolás Ovando, a company had been formed by the King and Ponce de León for the exploitation of the mines. After careful study and deliberation by both parties, the agreement had been corrected and then approved on the first and second of May 1509.

Ponce de León personally testified to what he had done since the moment he first arrived on August 12, 1508: that he had prepared the land, planted a crop of yucca (the bread of the land) and had later sold it amongst the Spaniards that were with him so that no one would steal the bread of the Indians. If they had need of the Indians' crops, the Spaniards either paid them a salary or bought the bread from the Indians. Ponce de León presented bills for expenses and an accounting of income earned from the sale of his crop.

On examination of the affairs of the company in the development of the mines, and considering the gold that had been extracted and melted, Sancho Velázquez sentenced Ponce on October 6, 1512, to pay one thousand, five hundred and thirty-two *pesos*, two *tomines* (one *tomin* is a third part of a *drachm*), and six grains of gold which belonged to the King and which Ponce de León had appropriated. Ponce protested officially and in writing before the royal treasurer, Francisco de Cardona, and García Troche, interim accountant. Sancho Velázquez confirmed his sentence on October 7, 1512, and asked for immediate payment. Ponce de León protestingly paid the money to the treasurer and appealed the sentence stating that he was deeply grieved. Sancho Velázquez officially discharged Ponce de León's heirs from any financial responsibility on October 10, 1512.

Continuing to maintain his innocence, Ponce de León waited patiently. At last, on March 3, 1519, Antonio de la Gama was named acting judge. The announcement of the second trial was made in the city of Puerto Rico on July 20, 1519. Ponce de León demanded the return of the moneys and gold that Sancho Velázquez had so injustly forced him to pay. De la Gama ordered Sancho Velázquez to return from his own purse the money he had so wrongly taken from Ponce de León.

All this previous information has been important in establishing where Ponce de León was in October 1512, and in disproving the malicious information given to Bartolomé de las Casas, who had believed the stories in good faith and had in 1516, as we have previously stated, passed on to Cardenal Cisneros information that, throughout the years, has detracted from the good name and honesty of Ponce de León.

"Pasamonte," says de las Casas, "subdelegated Sancho Velázquez to take an accounting of Ponce de León's affairs and bribed him with gifts."

"In a separate action, but as part of the same case, he sent Conchillos to examine Francisco de Lizaur's accounts. Lizaur paid him eight hundred gold marks and, when the affair was settled, asked for the money back. Both men argued, and then the falsity of the accounting was exposed."

This action of the first attorney general of the recently created Court of Santo Domingo, and special judge in the Ponce de León case is inexplicable. He seemed not to have learned from the previous warnings of the king, Don Fernando, nor from the punishment of Lizaur.

What really matters is that now Ponce de León was free to move around while waiting for the return from Castille of Iñigo de Zúñiga, who had been so successful in the court.

On December 10, 1512, Don Fernando wrote to the officials of the island of Hispaniola, "it is necessary that Juan Ponce de León be in charge of the royal lands and the distribution of the Indians on the island of San Juan, and so I have ordered the position of treasurer of this island to be given to him as well as the lieutenancy of the fortress that he built there."

Thus it was decreed that Juan Cerón ceased in his office of lieutenant governor, and Don Diego Colón named Rodrigo de Moscoso to succeed him. Moscoso arrived at the port of San Germán on December 27, 1513, in the ship *Santa María de la Consolación,* of which Juan Bono de Quejo was captain.

The moral and legal victory of Ponce de León was complete. The monarch had charged him with the economical administration and the defense of the island as well as the defense of the Indians. He could not give him the office of governor because it was in the hands of Don Diego Colón by court decree, but he did force Colón to change lieutenant governors.

Events of 1513

Don Diego Colón, together with Chief Mayor Marcos de Aguilar, Captain Enrique, and others, visited the island of San Juan while Ponce de León was away on a trip which would lead him to the discovery of Florida. During their stay in the town of San Germán, the Caribs invaded the island. Their line of march took them through the Daguao, around the Luquillo Mountains, through the Caguas Valley to the town of Caparra. Here, Ponce de León had built his home, first of adobe and later, when he was governor, of stone. Ponce de León's wife and children were living there when the Caribs attacked and burned the town. The house of Bishop Don Alonso Manso, the first bishop to arrive in the New Continent (December 25, 1512) was also destroyed, as was the church. Many Christians were wounded in this encounter.

Since Ponce de León was away on the voyage of discovery, he was unable to defend his town, nor to be beside his family. This is why he was so determined to punish the Caribs, at least the ones who kept attacking the island of San Juan. For this purpose he requested and was granted the use of the fleet. He personally returned the fleet to Seville in 1516.

Ponce de León never connected the killing of the Sotomayor party to the Caribs. This is why he did not take part in any way with the editing or carrying out of the royal decree in which these killings were used to legitimize the inhuman hunting down of all Indians and their enslavement under the pretext that they were cannibals, or cooperating with cannibals, or slaves of cannibals.

Reasons that Motivated Ponce de León to Embark Upon His Trip to the Land He Would Name Florida

Juan Ponce de León was free, in October 1512, to leave the island of San Juan and to go if he so wished to Hispaniola. The royal treasurer, Miguel de Pasamonte, had told Ponce de León in secret during the summer of 1511 about the existence of the island of Bimini. He then assisted Ponce in drawing up a contract for the exploration and development of Bimini in competition to a similar proposal by Bartolomé Colón. Don Fernando chose Ponce de León's bid over that of Don Bartolomé who had made, actually, a better offer.

The approval of the proposal for the discovery and colonization of the island of Bimini was issued on February 23, 1512, a day after the death of Américo Vespucio (Amerigo Vespucci).

Américo Vespucio had been granted citizenship of the kingdoms of Castille on April 24, 1505. Thus, a naturalized citizen participated in the exploration of these new lands much like other modern-day naturalized citizens would work in Florida to contribute to the exploration of space.

Américo Vespucio was named on March 22, 1508, chief navigator of the House of Trade in Seville, and received royal instructions on August 8, 1508, to examine all navigators as to their knowledge of the astrolobe, which they were all to carry with them on their voyages. He was also charged with making a general chart which would be known as the Royal Chart, "as the only means to organize the maps of the navigators and different shipmasters who were to participate in the exploration and colonization of the new lands."

It is logical to deduce that Américo Vespucio and Juan Vespucio (assistant to his uncle and heir to his nautical secrets) who had been appointed navigator on May 22, 1512, would intervene in the editing of the terms of the contract given to Ponce de León with regard to the course that he would follow to reach Bimini and its probable geographical location, "so as to make sure that it is not one of the islands previously discovered."

The first term of the agreement dealt with the route to Bimini: "...on your trip you may land upon any island or continental land of the Ocean Sea, discovered or to be discovered, as long as they are not islands or continental lands that belong to the most serene King of Portugal our dearly beloved son (King Manuel had married Isabel and after her death, María, both daughters of the monarchs Ferdinand and Isabel) according to

"Florida"

the agreement between us. Nor will you be able to take anything, nor profit in anyway from what is there, except for those provisions which might be needed for the maintenance of the ships and crew, paying for them according to their value."

There was nothing odd to this warning which was given to any one leaving from Castille or the Canary Islands, although never had there been such precise and specific information about the line of demarcation agreed upon in the Treaty of Tordesillas (June 7, 1494) between the ambassadors of the dual monarchs and their neighbor, King Juan II of Portugal. The line of partition began 370 leagues west of the Cape Verde Islands, and ran north to south from the Arctic to the Antarctic. Any lands between the Cape Verdes and the demarcation line belonged to Portugal and from there on to the kings of Castille and Aragón. The group of astronomers, mathematicians, and navigators from both sides had been given ten months in which to accomplish the establishment of the demarcation. Of course, the Spaniards would have to cross the Portuguese portion to arrive at the line and this right was granted.

The island of San Juan (later named Puerto Rico) had been discovered by Columbus (Colón) on November 17-19, 1493. With the arrival of Ponce de León on August 12, 1508, the second Spanish colony in the New World began. The first colony had been established in Hispaniola. The island of San Juan became a strategic base because of its geographical location. There was never any doubt that the island of San Juan was well within the Spanish area. On Ponce de León's journey to Bimini and the other adjacent islands he would travel north in order to explore the Hispaniola Gulf and look for a strait. Previously on March 23, 1508, Juan de Solís and Vicente Yañez Pinzón had made an unsuccessful attempt. The King had told them, "I want you to find a channel or open sea, for if not, I would be greatly displeased and I will have you punished as best I see fit."

The trip was urgent, and Don Fernando ordered the chartering of ships for three months with all the necessary provisions including medicines and a surgeon. The trip, according to legal documents, accounts, and royal decrees, lasted a year, from July 1508 to August 1509, for they stopped here and there discovering new lands from Veragua (discovered by Columbus on his fourth journey) on to the north, but they did not discover the channel nor the open sea. Don Fernando ordered the punishment of Pinzón and Solís. They requested Miguel de Pasamonte for their defense lawyer, since on his own return trip he had stopped at Hispaniola and was well informed of the events of the Pinzón and Solís expedition. Pasamonte's information must have been favorable because on March 20, 1510, Don Fernando ordered the expenses incurred on the trip paid up to August 29, 1509.

On March 2, 1510, Ponce de León had been appointed captain governor of the island of San Juan, and the first royal letter addressed to him as such on April 4, 1510, orders him to give to Vicente Yañez Pinzón, "our navigator, for services well rendered," one hundred Indian slaves, and on the ninth of April another letter orders him to give to Pinzón 768 acres (8 *caballerías*) on the island of San Juan. The land had originally been promised to Pinzón on April 24, 1505, but had never been given to him.

Neither Pinzón nor Solís claimed any rights in the newly discovered lands, nor did don Fernando show any interest in them. Both men went on to serve in the House of Trade in Seville. Solís was installed as chief navigator on March 25, 1512, after this post had been vacated by the death of Américo Vespucio, and Juan Vespucio, Américo's nephew, was appointed navigator. They were both charged on July 24, 1512, to prepare a general chart for which they were, "to gather all the navigators who knew the most about navigating, astrolobes, measurements and compasses... because I have found out that there are many charts of the same areas prepared in different ways by shipmasters, in which the locations of the lands of the Indies, and the islands and continental lands of the ocean sea, that belong to us differ. The routes to be taken to them also differ, as does the information about settlements in them."

Solís felt obligated to Don Fernando and so, two days after his appointment (March 27, 1512) when he received a contract to undertake a trip around the Cape of Good Hope, he accepted. "For the purpose of arriving in China. I charge you with God and your conscience, to follow the demarcation line in such a way that both parties may be pleased." The trip was to try to find some route other than through the Hispaniola Gulf to the open sea or a channel: the antemeridian of the demarcation line made on a planisphere.

The multiplicity of divergent maps were actually drawn on a sphere or globe, an accepted configuration, but this knowledge was totally overlooked in practice and the obligation of having to organize all that confusion on a plane surface was difficult at best. Added to this was the lack of precise measurements and the lack of a uniform scale. Under these conditions, to try to prepare a general chart was enough to challenge the mind of the one who accepted the royal commission or to drive him insane. Méndez Vasconcellos, the Portuguese ambassador, learned of the interview between Solís and the King and made use of this opportunity to ask Solís to return to the service of the king of Portugal. Solís excused himself, informing the ambassador of his appointment and the commission of Don Fernando, a double honor. Vasconcellos notified the king of Portugal of the events and the Portuguese king denied Solís a pass for the trip. Vasconcellos informed Don Fernando of the royal decision. Don Fernando expressed his sorrow and asked Vasconcellos to so express it to the king of Portugal. The Ambassador did this in a letter to Don Manuel, dated September 9, 1512, " ... in the House of Trade of Seville, the principal regulation given to those undertaking discovery journeys (read the contract given to Ponce de León) was that they would not lay hands on anything belonging to Your Highness ... ; that he, Don Fernando, was truly interested in honoring the line of demarcation so that Portugal and Castille would never have any differences; he emphasized this to me and asked me to write Your Highness to see if there was someway to carry out the trip because this decision would make him very happy. He said he was old and should not live long, and that he asked God that there would never be a disagreement, for he would die more peacefully if he could leave matters well settled so that his grandchildren and their descendants would never have to break any agreements. That he would be well pleased with this." Don Fernando's intention, so stated to the ambassador, casts a favorable light on the monarch.

Don Fernando ordered on September 30, 1512, the cancellation of Solís' trip. Solís continued in Seville working on the squaring of the circle, the General Chart, without ever giving up his dream, which he tried once more to carry out on November 24, 1514. He proposed to place three ships, "on the other side of Castilla del Oro" (opposite what is now called the Gulf of Darién) by traveling from the line of demarcation that goes through the tip of the above mentioned Castilla del Oro, one thousand, seven hundred leagues or more. To reach that point (today a port in Panama), he would travel along the newly discovered coastline in the southern Atlantic, which Spain had a right to use, in search of the strait to the Southern Ocean that Magellan later discovered in November 1520. Solís died on the trip in 1516, a victim of the Indians. Solís had tried to merge in this trip the common purpose and the two routes of the previously planned and frustrated trips: to find the antemeridian.

Don Fernando did not value the lands discovered by Pinzón and Solís in their attempt to discover the strait or the open sea which would provide

Spain with a way out of its confinement in the Gulf of Hispaniola. His attitude is obvious from his communique to Don Diego Colón on December 10, 1512, " ... in order to colonize Veragua and all the lands discovered by Admiral Christopher Columbus (Colón) and to colonize the lands discovered by Vicente Yañez Pinzón and Juan Díaz de Solís and to carry out the complete exploration of the Gulf of Hispaniola in order to discover the strait, as many have attempted to do, you may act without consulting us, so as to save time if you think that it is to our service."

Miguel de Pasamonte informed Ponce de León about the exploration license requested by Don Diego. Don Diego did not include Bimini for he knew of Ponce de León's contract. Nevertheless, Ponce de León ran into Diego Miruelo close to Bimini.

Pasamonte reminded Ponce of Don Bartolomé Colón's offer to undertake the discovery of Bimini, and therefore of the need to carry out the planned trip as soon as possible before the end of the year stipulated in the royal contract which all would honor. Pasamonte was the only one who could replace Ponce de León in the official responsibilities on the island of San Juan, which Don Fernando had granted to Ponce in demonstration of his good will. Pasamonte helped him prepare for the trip: the ship *Santa María de la Consolación*, captained by Juan Bono de Quejo, had arrived at San Germán, island of San Juan, bringing the lieutenant governor, Don Rodrigo Moscoso, with all his retinue on December 27, 1512. A month later, with Ponce de León on board, the ship and its captain departed for the discovery of Bimini.

Ponce de León's Itinerary on his Trip to Florida

I have been following the footsteps of Ponce de León for forty years. I found the original documents of Ponce de León's departure from the port of Yuma, in the township of Salvaleón, province of Higüey, on the island of Hispaniola on January 29, 1513. Ponce de León sailed on the ship *María de la Consolación*, captained by Juan Bono de Quejo. Accompanying them was the ship *Santiago*, captained by Diego Bermúdez with Antón de Alaminos as navigator. On their Bimini journey of discovery, they first stopped at the island of San Juan on February 8. The names of all the persons on both ships are given in the documents. On the island of San Juan, Ponce de León prepared and supplied the caravel *San Cristóbal*, which was captained by Juan Pérez de Ortubia.

The three ships left from the port of San Germán for Aguada, a nearby spot, from which they set out on March 3, 1513. From this date on, Antonio de Herrera, the chronicler, begins his description, giving details of the trip. He narrates the events leading to September 23, hurriedly, as if he would want to quickly end this chapter. He gives the following significant facts: (1) "The ship from Hispaniola with Diego Miruelo as pilot, that had joined the expedition on July 25, was shipwrecked and all hands were saved; (2) Ponce de León decided to return to San Juan, which he did on September 18, but (3) a day before, on September 17, he sent Capt. Juan Pérez de Ortubia and the pilot Antón de Alaminos to discover Bimini, which they did. They did not however, discover the fountain which the Indians claimed turned old men young. It took Ponce de León twenty-one days to arrive at the bay of Puerto Rico. Ortubia and Alaminos arrived later."

Herrera claims that the expedition dissolved on the island of Guatao-Curatheo, but only the survivors of the shipwreck were there on September 23, 1513.

As to the discovery of Bimini, I found an original document which I photocopied and published in my before-mentioned book, *Juan Ponce de León*, and which I am including here in its totality: "A report on the Indians that were brought over in the caravel *San Cristóbal*, which anchored in the port of San Germán on February 20, 1514, and which was navigated by Antón de Alaminos, who had just discovered the island of Bimini in the name of Juan Ponce de León, by order of his Highness and by that of his captain, Juan Pérez de Ortubia, and also on the Indians brought from the island of Bimini and from other neighboring islands is as follows: (1) From Bimini they brought four Indians whose Christian names were Antón, Alonso, Hernando, and Simón, but only three arrived, for Simón died on the way. (2) They brought from Cignateo, an island in the Lucayos, six Indians: two men, three boys, and a woman with a baby.

"Juan Pérez de Ortubia, captain of the vessel, solemnly swore that he had taken nothing else from Bimini or any of the other islands that he explored, nor any ransom, nor anything that belonged to the King."

Pérez de Ortubia and the pilot Alaminos discovered Bimini and other islands in the name of Ponce de León, and they returned to San Germán on February 20, 1514, from where they had departed on March 3, 1513.

Ponce de León had anchored in the bay of Puerto Rico in October 1513, four months before Ortubia and Alaminos. On the return trip, Ponce de León called on some of the islands previously discovered and arrived at the island of Guanahaní, where he got provisions for his ships, on March

14, 1513. We do not know how long he remained there, but we do know that he departed on a northwesterly route. On Sunday the twenty-seventh, which was Easter Sunday, commonly known, Herrera states, as the "Flowered" (or Flowered Paschal) in the documents of that time, they saw an island which Ponce de León named Florida *(La Florida)*. Garcilaso de la Vega, "the Inca," categorically states that it was in the year 1513.

Concerning the route taken by Ponce de León to Florida, there was a certain error brought about by the writings of the celebrated humanist and historian, Pedro Mártir de Anglería, a naturalized Spaniard from Milan. He had published in the *First Decades of the New World, 1511*, a map in which he placed Bimini in the location of Florida. Anglería was a confidant of Bishop Rodríguez de Fonseca, zealous guardian of cartographic secrets. We would like to remind the reader of the previously mentioned secret which Ponce de León had heard from Pasamonte and he in turn from Pinzón and Solís, who in 1509 had given an account of their trip to Américo Vespucio, chief navigator of the House of Trade. Through Vespucio, the information had passed on to the secret archives of Bishop Fonseca.

On the map that we published of the gulfs of Hispaniola and of Mexico, the only one of its time preserved in the Archives of the Indies (1520?), drawn upon request of Ponce de León while Sebastián Caboto was chief navigator of the House of Trade in Seville, there is a circle around the peninsula labeled Florida and handwritten beside the name is the message, "previously thought to be Bimini." Experts could determine whether it is Caboto's handwriting. This clearly points out the error of Anglería.

From March 27 to June 11, if we follow the itinerary, Ponce de León occupied himself with the land and sea exploration of Florida, fearing no dangers, not even the forbidding ocean currents (so strong that today they have become a possible source of energy). As to the exact location of the places visited by Ponce de León, I submit to the authority of the Florida historians, to whom I wish success in their excavation which may lead to interesting findings. Here I only want to mention the naming of a river, Cross *(Cruz)*, and a carved stone cross with an inscription. This probably coincided with the traditional Spanish festivity of the Cross, celebrated on May 3. Herrera includes this date but gives no details. Today, I have been told, one can still find the spot, close to Jupiter Light.

Two Symbols: Easter Sunday, or Flowered Paschal, and the Cross Unquestionably Represent Christianity; and they also Represent the United States of America in its Bicentennial Celebration

Ponce de León and Juan Pérez de Ortubia arrived at Bayona de Mier, Galicia, in April 1514. They gave a complete account of the discovery of Florida to Solís, chief navigator at the House of Trade in Seville, in compliance with the royal specifications dictated when Américo Vespucio was first appointed. At that time, working for the House of Trade were Juan Vespucio, naval cartographer Vicente Yañez Pinzón, and Sebastián Caboto. On October 20, 1512, Caboto had been appointed captain in the service of Spain but assigned to English ships, for at that time Henry VIII and Don Fernando were allies in the Italian conflict. Upon his return from his assignment, Caboto joined the trading company and was working there as navigator towards the middle of March 1514. They were all to receive the happy news of the discovery of the new lands and to try to place them on the General Chart. Don Diego Colón also heard of the new discoveries but did not make any claims to them in spite of the continued antagonism between him and Ponce de León. Don Fernando must have ratified Ponce de León's claim, for on September 27, 1514, he ordered Ponce de León to colonize the islands of Bimini and Florida and gave him the title of governor of these islands, "which you have discovered and the other islands or lands that in that region you may discover by our command and which have not yet been discovered by anyone else."

It so happened that the news of the discovery of an "open sea" named the Southern Sea by the famous Vasco Núñez de Balboa on September 25, 1513, got to Castille in August 1514 in a letter from Miguel de Pasamonte. Pasamonte sent two letters with the news about Balboa's discovery dated March 12, 1514. Magellan would, in 1520, rediscover the same sea and name it the Pacific. Don Fernando gave the title of Governor of the Southern Sea to Vasco Núñez de Balboa on September 23, 1514.

Ponce de León received his and Balboa's appointments in Valladolid on September 30, 1514, and personally delivered these documents to the House of Trade. While there, he met with Solís, Vicente Yáñez Pinzón, Juan Vespucio, and Sebastián Caboto to celebrate the discoveries of the two governors—Balboa, of the Southern Sea, and Juan Ponce de León, of the Northern Lands. (I will leave my readers who are interested in such turns of history to their own thoughts).

Towards the End of 1514, while Ponce de León was still in Castille, a Caravel with Eleven Portuguese was Captured Off the Island of San Juan

On February 10, 1515, Don Fernando ordered Don Diego Colón and the appeal judges at Hispaniola to send to Seville the eleven captured Portuguese, and at the same time he wrote to the officers of the House of Trade to carefully investigate the matter so as to make sure that his agreement with the king of Portugal had not been violated.

On October 11, 1515, as we have previously stated, Solís left from Sanlúcar for a trip along the southern shore of the discovered lands (the Atlantic coast of South America) to get behind Castilla del Oro on the shores of the Southern Sea and from here to go in search for the antimeridian. Don Fernando, in reply to a letter (October 15, 1515) from the officers of the House of Trade, wrote, "I am very pleased with the successful departure of Juan de Solís... you should always request the prayers of the monasteries of the city in behalf of the affairs of the Indies and especially for journeys such as the one undertaken by Juan de Solís and others...

"I have seen your report on the eleven captured Portuguese... this partition matter is of such importance that it will be the determining factor in the case of the Portuguese, for the King of Portugal might want to take advantage of our decision in determining the boundary of the partition between our kingdoms, and before a final decision is reached it is of great importance that all the facts be known about the negotiation. It would certainly be beneficial if Juan de Solís were here because of his knowledge of navigation, but since this can not be, you are to put together, besides all that you already have, all that you know about the art of navigation... and since Juan de Solís and others approved the map made by Andrés Morales, and believed it was the best, send me immediately upon receipt of my letter by foot messenger the partition that you tell me you have come up with that can be of use in these negotiations."

Soon after this letter, he wrote on November 27, 1515, in response to a letter (October 30) from the officers of the House of Trade, "I am aware of the care you have taken to question each and every one of the navigators on their opinion about the position of the Cape of Saint Augustine to see if the captured Portuguese were within our demarcation lines. It is important to have their opinions and yours which I have read in your letter, so that after careful thought we may do what is best."

Solís was killed by Indians at the mouth of the La Plata River (the border of present-day Argentina and Uruguay), which he had discovered towards the end of January or early February 1516. Solís' companions on this journey, deciding to return to Seville, sailed along the shore on the return trip. Off the island of Santa Catalina one of the ships was lost and seven crew members remained there shipwrecked. They were captured by the Portuguese and taken to Lisbon. Cardinal Cisneros, regent of Spain, wrote to the officers of the House of Trade on March 30, 1517, telling them, "I have written to the King of Portugal proposing the exchange of the seven Spaniards that were in Solís' expedition for the eleven Portuguese captured on the island of San Juan."

We should here examine for a moment Don Fernando's far-reaching goal, his perseverance and his tenacity in carrying it out, all of which came to a head in the capture of the Portuguese on the island of San Juan. His goal was exploration and scientific measuring, by instrument, of the earth as a globe. This concept had been established by Columbus (Colón) but was ignored in practice. Here was the reason for the multiplicity of routes taken to fulfill the exploration contracts. At this time there was nothing to be gained in sitting down at a round-table discussion about the line of demarcation or the partition of lands discovered or to be discovered.

As to the possible spice trade, it served as a pretext to keep the secret and to console the exhausted discoverer, Columbus, and not hasten his death. Because of this and the affection Columbus had for Hispaniola, the agreement of 1505 was made, assigning the island of San Juan to Vicente Yáñez Pinzón as a base of operations. It was ratified as such with the departure of Ponce de León from San Juan on his journey to discover Florida, and finally recognized with the capture of the Portuguese who had landed on the island. From that time, toward the end of 1514, the Portuguese and Spaniards pressed on to accomplish the scientific measuring of the globe in degrees of longitude and latitude, always allowing for possible corrections.

Ponce de León, Captain of the Fleet against the Caribs and Captain-General of the Island of San Juan

Both of the above stated appointments as well as his designation as governor of Florida were made on the same date, September 27, 1514. Thus, the monarch, Don Fernando, had decided that the personal direction of Ponce de León was needed in two strategic locations.

Ponce de León knew of the fleet organized at Hispaniola. That is why he purposely avoided getting involved in the inhuman hunting down of Indians so as to bring them and sell them as slaves at Hispaniola under the pretext of pursuing the Caribs or cannibals, who according to the slave traders carried the curse of having killed the Sotomayor party. Ponce de León had time to carefully consider the burning of his beloved home at Caparra by the Caribs while he was away on his voyage of discovery. He felt that the hunting down of these Indians in their lands and homes was an incitement to further reprisals. The royal treasurer of San Juan, Andrés de Haro, wrote about the invasion of three hundred Caribs; it is difficult to believe the exhorbitant number quoted when one reads on in the next line that he was requesting additional ships for the fleet and more slave traders. Ponce de León decided to proceed with his own plans, preferring to be captain of his own fleet, with the three old ships acquired by the House of Trade and loaned to him equipped with the surplus of the great fleet under the command of Pedrarías Dávila. Ponce de León left Seville the fourteenth of May 1515. He stopped in the Canary Islands and at the island of Guadalupe, where the Indians wounded some of the Spaniards. Ponce de León loaded the wounded into the ships, and lifted anchor without slaughtering or enslaving the Indians, an action which Anglería claims was dishonorable. He arrived safe and sound in San Juan on July 25, 1515.

As captain of a fleet he could continue to act independently while on land and was not summoned to appear in court, but he had to respect the routes of other fleets and he was ordered by royal decree to go "immediately" to the islands of the Caribs from which they ventured forth to attack the island of San Juan.

I have published some lists of the Indian women and children of the island of San Juan rescued by the fleet of Governor Ponce de León and of the delivery of other Indians, men and women, to the royal officers for them to decide whether these Indians were former slaves or not. Not knowing if the Indians were former slaves or not, the men of Ponce de

"Florida"

León's fleet treated them with respect. The biggest problem was the maintenance of the men, who were not on salary. They were to receive a certain percentage of the value of the cargo, the appraisal of which depended on the royal officers who had interests in other fleets. Ponce de León asked the King to allow him to take charge and the King agreed. But the King died on January 23, 1516, before the royal decree was signed and put into practice.

The change in command coincided with a moment of great restlessness in the Indies. Cardinal Cisneros, governor of the Kingdoms, personally intervened in the problem which he considered a matter of conscience. He appointed as commissioners three priests from the order of Saint Geronimo. They departed from Sanlúcar on November 11, 1516; they stopped at Gomera and proceeded to San Juan. Ponce de León was not there; he was in Seville (November 16) where on November 27 he handed over two of the three ships he had been loaned, the third ship having been returned to the officers at Hispaniola. He liquidated all his accounts with Dr. Matienzo, treasurer of the House of Trade. By order of Cardinal Cisneros, he received the "finiquito" or satisfaction of debts for his heirs on July 30, 1517. Later on December 6, 1524, Francisco Velázquez, special royal accountant, demanded from García Troche, testamentory executor and son-in-law of Juan Ponce de León, proof of the expenses and payments for the fleet which pursued the Caribs. There are no references made of the expenses of a possible trip to Florida and other places. On September 27, 1514, in confirmation and enlargement of Ponce de León's contract for Florida, Don Fernando had authorized Ponce, upon completion of the mission against the Caribs, to return to Florida. This voyage is probably the trip Lope de Gomara talks about and passes on to other historians.

In Seville, Ponce de León protested vigorously to the governors of the Kingdoms that Diego Velázquez, lieutenant governor of Cuba, Indian hunter and enslaver, had sent an expedition to the islands of Bimini and Florida and had captured three hundred Indians, which was a breach of his contract. Cardinal Cisneros transferred the case to the three priests, commissioners of the Indies, on July 22, 1517.

The office of captain general of the island of San Juan was granted to Ponce de León for life. He discharged this duty from 1514 to his death in 1521. It was given to him, "so that the rebelling Indians may be more quickly pacified, and there may be less damage and deaths than what have occurred up to now, and so that they will not rebel in the future." This royal decree was directed to the Council of Magistrates and to aldermen of the cities, towns, and villages of San Juan, and Ponce could discharge his duty either directly or through his deputies. "I order the councils," said the King, "to swear in Ponce and to cooperate with him in all that he esteems necessary for the security and appeasement of the island." The royal decree was directed to all the councils of the island and they were to receive him as Captain General, a title that made reference to the territory under his command, his jurisdiction, and the power he had to appoint deputies. Ponce de León discharged his duties during the government of Sancho Velázquez and his successor, Antonio de la Gama, and during the second government of the Viceroy Diego Colón. Ponce de León was never sworn in by the governor of the island. We can confirm that he was the first captain general of the Indies with military authority independent of the governor or the chief justice and with direct contact with the people (as is stated in the royal decree) through the municipal councils. When Ponce de León embarked once more for Florida in 1521, he legally delegated his authority to García Troche and Cristóbal Maldonado.

The Fountain of Youth in Florida: Ponce de León Marries a Young Girl of Seville

Ponce de León and the fountain of youth have been the subject of all kinds of literary works such as legends, stories, poetry, theater scripts, and jokes. It is a delightful, attractive, and economical means of publicity which should be continued and augmented in order to make the man and the place known. In the history books and dictionaries which one may consult to verify the historical truth of the events, it is another matter. Ponce de León did not set out in search of the fountain of youth in Bimini, which he never visited, nor in Florida which he discovered, named, and where, years later, he was mortally wounded.

Ponce de León declared in Valladolid on September 28th, 1514, to the mayor of the royal court that he was forty years of age; on the twenty-third of September 1519, in San Juan, he declared to Judge Antonio de la Gama that he was fifty years of age.

On two occasions he gave his age incorrectly, but not officially, for he was not obliged to state his exact age but only to declare that he was of legal age. Today we still do not know with certainty who his parents were or when he was born, for there are no legal documents or papers to be found. He was born in Santervás de Campos which is in the province of

Valladolid between the kingdoms of León and Castille. We know that he came to the Indies with Columbus (Colón) on his second trip, and perhaps because of illness returned to Spain. He came back with Fr. Nicolás Ovando (1502), and he was appointed captain of the troops (1504) that left the city of Santo Domingo, on the island of Hispaniola to subdue the Indians in the province of Higüey. Ovando authorized the establishment of two towns, one which was Salvaleón, and appointed Ponce de León deputy of the province of Higüey. Here Ponce built a home which has been recently restored by the government of the Dominican Republic. On June 15, 1508, he signed a contract with Ovando to establish a company with the King for the settlement of the island of San Juan. He landed with fifty men on August 12. In May 1509, they revised and renewed the contract and Ponce de León brought to the island his wife, Leonor Ponce de León, his son Luis, and his three daughters, Juana, Isabel, and María. Juana was married in September 1519 to García Troche; Isabel married, in 1520, Gov. Antonio de la Gama; and María married Gaspar Troche, brother of García.

Juan Ponce de León, Governor of Bimini and Florida, Married Juana de Pineda in Seville in 1517 or the Beginning of 1518

In Seville on August 8, 1520, Diego Melgarejo, father of Juana de Pineda, authorized Fr. Juan González to represent him in the court of the city of Santo Domingo and the island of San Juan in his lawsuit against Gov. Juan Ponce de León with regard to the dowry received from his daughter, Juana de Pineda, the governor's wife. The lawsuit was still going on in the Court of Appeals in Seville against the governor's heirs in 1536. It was there on August 20, 1536, that Diego Melgarejo requested the confiscation of Juan Ponce de León's 202,000 *maravedís*, which were in the hands of Don Luis Cristóbal Ponce de León, Duke of Arcos.

Alonso Pérez Martel from San Juan, who had married Leonor, a daughter of García Troche and Juana Ponce and granddaughter of Juan Ponce de León, intervened in behalf of the heirs, and together with Diego Melgarejo, distributed the money, pending final approval of the court. What has been said should suffice to prove beyond doubt the second marriage of Florida's governor. Through this marriage, family ties were established with the house of the Duke of Arcos; ties which were later more closely interwoven by the marriage of Alonso Pérez Martel and Ponce de León's granddaughter.

Doña Francisca Ponce de León, Marchioness of Zahara, gave power of attorney in Seville in 1518 to her cousin Juan Ponce de León, the governor of Bimini and Florida. Cousin then meant relative, especially if no degree of family closeness was indicated. When the judge asked García Troche (September 24, 1519) if he was related to any of the contesting parties in the case of Ponce de León versus Velázquez, García Troche answered that he was a relative of Velázquez four times removed, but that he was not related to the other party. Three days later when he testified, he said he was Ponce de León's son-in-law.

Ponce de León is Wounded by the Indians in Florida in 1521

Ponce de León returned to the island of San Juan with his young wife in May 1518. The commissioner priests ordered the retroactive payment of his salary as captain general and showed him both personal and public honor.

The commissioners granted a license to Antonio de Sedeño to provision three ships and a brigantine to search for the gulf or strait in 1518.

In 1519, they gave permission to Francisco Garay to provision four ships and to also search for the gulf. These privateers sailed for eight or nine months but they never discovered the gulf or the strait. They did, however, come up Florida, already discovered by Juan Ponce de León, and then they turned back till they reached the land of Hernán Cortés. They covered from one to the other about three hundred leagues. Garay asked the monarch for a contract to colonize the territory, which the monarch granted. He, nevertheless, stipulated that the limits had to be verified by Cristóbal de Tapia, royal overseer in Diego Velázquez's fleet. An account of the discoveries, in compliance to the royal decree, had to be given to the chief navigator, who at that time was Sebastian Caboto.

Ponce de León postponed his departure for Florida because of the death of his young Sevillian wife. This lady was not the mother of his children, as many have thought.

On February 10, 1521, he wrote a simple, brief, and expressive letter, which is still preserved, to the Emperor Charles I, in which he said, "I am returning to that island, Florida, which I discovered at my expense and the willingness of God (1) to colonize it with a group of able people (2) that they may there praise the NAME OF GOD (3) and so that Your Majesty may be well served with the fruits that this land may bear, (4) and to decide

"Florida"

whether to explore further the coast of this island, if island it is, or (5) to determine if it is bound to the land of Diego Velázquez or any other.

"I leave from here on my trip in five days. Of what we see and do in those parts I will write to Your Majesty upon my return. Island of San Juan, city of Puerto Rico." (It is signed Juan Ponce de León).

A few days earlier, on January 25, 1521, Ponce de León appointed his deputies on the island of San Juan. He was thinking of maintaining his ties with San Juan while colonizing Florida.

The mortal wounds inflicted while in Florida (it is not known for certain whether this happened on land or on ship); the death of Ponce in the town of San Cristóbal, Havana; and the confiscation of the ships and their cargo by the mayor of Havana bring out a series of questions. In the royal *cédulas,* (decrees) of July 4, 1523, and November 6, 1524, these facts were presented by the heirs of Ponce de León. These facts are important considering the lawsuit of the father of Ponce de León's young wife who in 1520 claimed the dowry of his daughter.

Juan Troche Ponce de León, a grandson, in the statement given in the city of San Juan of Puerto Rico on April 9, 1550, to Governor Vallejo requested that the witnesses answer the following question (listed as No. 6): "Item—if they know that in the so-called conquest of Florida, Juan Ponce de León, my grandfather, and his nephew, Hernán Ponce, with some of their followers disembarked to explore the land and communicate with the Indians and attract them to the service of his majesty. They also wanted to find out if there was gold there. While they were talking to the Indians, the Indians killed them. In that way Ponce de León died. After his death, the union was lost." (Juan Ponce de León II is the one who asked the question and who transferred the Governor's remains from Havana to the city of San Juan in Puerto Rico where they have remained in the Cathedral.)

Edward W. Lawson, the erudite author of *The Discovery of Florida and its Discoverer, Juan Ponce de León* (Saint Augustine, Florida, 1946) maintains that Ponce de León and the Spaniards did land.

Did they at least set up camp? If they did, how many days did they remain in Florida? The first operation performed on Ponce de León, was it on land? Was the operation successful enough so that he was alive when he arrived in Havana? Were they able to plant the seeds they had taken? Did they leave some behind?

Florida's historians truly interested in Ponce de León will hopefully someday, after deeper investigations, answer some of these questions.

Meanwhile, I continue working on my book *The Island of San Juan and Florida in the XVI Century,* and on my studies of the people that intervened in both places.

MOSAIC OF TRADITIONAL CULTURE
by R. S. Boggs

Principles of traditional culture

Man is gregarious by nature, hence he lives in groups, not isolated and alone. The association of people forms the community. In the course of time, these individuals who live and work together develop their manner of thinking, speaking, and acting, which results from their adaptation to their environment and the interaction which occurs among them. This *modus vivendi* gradually gains the approval of the majority of the community.

If some members of this group move to another region, their traditional culture becomes modified to harmonize with their new environment as a result of interaction with the traditional culture of the people already living in the new region. When different groups live together, the traditional culture of each group exerts influence on that of the other. Generally that of the larger group exerts greater influence, though that of the smaller group can predominate if it is more powerful and dominates the larger group with which it lives. When two groups live together, each one tries to keep together and somewhat isolated from the other in order to preserve its culture and language; but finally cultural fusion inevitably takes place.

These principles and others can be seen in the state of Florida, which in the last half millennium of documented history has received an influx of population of such diverse origins that Florida traditional culture as a whole appears like a many-colored mosaic, or a revolving kaleidoscope if viewed through its history, because traditional culture, like all living things, is constantly changing.

The People

In order to know traditional culture, one must know its bearers. In the sixteenth- and seventeenth-century chronicles we learn that all Florida was populated by Indians because, from the beginning, explorers found them all along the Atlantic coast and along the coast of the Gulf of Mexico. Treated badly by the Europeans, these Indians almost disappeared. Their last refuge was that most inaccessible region, the huge swamps in the interior of the southern part of the peninsula: around Lake Okeechobee, Big Cypress Swamp, and the Everglades.

The *modern Seminole Indians* seem to have little relation and continuity of traditional culture with the sixteenth-century Indians. Their origin is obscure. It is said that around 1750 a few hundred Creek Indians of Georgia, discontented there, migrated to the south and joined some surviving Florida Indians, the Miccosukee, in defending themselves against their common enemy, the European. The United States took possession of Florida in 1821, dislodging the poor Indians from their lands, and began a war in 1835. In 1837 the great Seminole warrior chief, Osceola, was captured, and in 1841 the tribe was moved to Oklahoma. But some one hundred fifty hid in the southern swamps, where more than a thousand of their descendants still survive, some of which say that their war with the United States has never ended, because they never signed a peace treaty.

It is true that some live very isolated in their swamps and maintain their own traditional culture, free of outside influences accepted by many others, including Christianity and government help in their economic development; and they have exploited tourism with the picturesque aspect of their primitive life along the Tamiami Trail and in Dania.

The so-called Cow Creek Seminoles, who speak a dialect of the Creek Indians, live within and around the Brighton reservation, on the north side of Lake Okeechobee. The Miccosukees, who speak a Hichi dialect, live within and around the reservations of the state, in Big Cypress Swamp and Dania, and along the Tamiami Trail.

The first European immigrants were the *Spanish*. In 1513, Juan Ponce de León, in search of the legendary fountain of youth, landed near the St. Augustine inlet. In 1528, Pánfilo de Narváez came ashore near Tampa Bay. In 1565, Pedro Menéndez de Avilés defeated the French Huguenots, who had settled on the banks of the St. Johns River near Jacksonville, and founded St. Augustine, the oldest city in the United States, seat of government for all the Spanish possessions of Florida and the coast of Georgia. In 1679, the Spanish built a fort at San Marcos de Apalache and further west on the Gulf of Mexico. In 1698, they established a permanent settlement at Pensacola to govern the western part of Florida. Pensacola underwent seventeen changes of government, being ruled by Spain, France, England, the Confederate States, and the United States; and under a weak Spanish government in the early nineteenth century it even became a base for Indian attacks against the white settlements of Georgia.

St. Augustine continued as capital of eastern Florida. When Spain ceded Florida to England in 1763, there began a period of twenty years of prosperity which won the support of the Floridians for England during the American Revolution, and St. Augustine became a refuge for the loyalists who fled from the adjacent southern colonies. When Florida was returned to Spain in 1783, many Americans moved into the houses and plantations abandoned by the English, encouraged by the Spanish.

Spain handed over Florida to the United States in 1821 and, in 1823, a single, log-cabin-style state capital was erected in Tallahassee, a place which the government bought from the Indians. When the English took possession of Florida in 1763, a large part of the Spanish population moved over to Cuba. Although several thousand were still remaining in 1821 when Florida became part of the United States, during the next half century the Spanish population decreased while the Anglo-American population increased. From 1868, because of the Cuban revolt against Spain, many Cubans arrived at Key West, which was established as a naval station in 1822.

Tampa was founded in 1824 and its importance as a commercial center was assured in the 1880s with the arrival of the railroad and the tobacco industry, plagued with labor trouble in Key West and because of the Cubans' struggle against Spain in Havana. Invited by Tampa, Vicente Martínez Ybor, Cuban cigar manufacturer, moved his factory and many of his employees in 1886 from Key West to some land on the eastern edge of Tampa, a place which acquired the name of Ybor City. With its tile roofs, balconies, grilles, and Spanish-Cuban cooking it still today preserves its own character, although now it is completely surrounded by the city of Tampa. Other cigar factories and many Spaniards, Cubans, and other Spanish-speaking people came so that, by around 1890, Ybor City had become a flourishing colony of these people. To this was added a quite large Italian population, and there Latin traditional culture prospered during half a century.

In the 1930s, the economic depression came, along with the mechanization of the cigar factories and the concentration of the tobacco industry in New York, New Jersey, and Pennsylvania, plus the expansion of Tampa on all sides of Ybor City, which as time goes on makes its assimilating influence felt.

In the second quarter of the twentieth century, Miami developed as the most important center in the United States for air communication with the countries of Hispanic America, and all these have contributed to its population; especially, in the beginning, Cubans and Puerto Ricans. In the third quarter of the twentieth century, with the oppression of the Communist government in Cuba, thousands and thousands of Cuban refugees have been arriving at Miami, where they have been very cordially received by the residents as they established themselves in certain neighborhoods and scattered throughout the city, dedicating themselves to all sorts of business. The Hispanic population of Miami proper, with its recent Cuban majority, now totals several hundred thousands. The Spaniards came in the sixteenth to eighteenth centuries. Hispanic Americans have been arriving since the last part of the nineteenth century. There is little continuity of traditional culture between these two periods.

After the Spaniards the *English* came. As we have seen, when Spain ceded Florida to England in 1763, many loyalists came from the neighboring southern colonies, fleeing the American Revolution, and they were followed by many Anglo-Americans, with the approval of the Spaniards, when Florida was returned to Spain in 1783. Since 1821, when Spain handed over Florida to the United States, the Anglo-American immigration has been continuous and the Anglo-American traditional culture is the most deeply rooted in Florida, especially in its Southern form; especially from Georgia, the nearest state. There is a folkloric nickname for the inhabitants of every state. The natives of Georgia and Florida have the same nickname: cracker. This is one proof of the unity of traditional culture of the two states.

Florida became a state in 1845. It joined the other Southern states in the Civil War, separating from the Northern government in 1861, and suffering through the Reconstruction period with the other Southern states. Anglo-Americans first populated the northern part of Florida from Pensacola to Jacksonville and St. Augustine, where their traditional culture is most deeply rooted in its Southern form. In the early twentieth century, the modern development of the state began with the extension of railroads

Mosaic of Traditional Culture

through the central part of the peninsula to Tampa and along the Atlantic coast to Key West. There continued an enormous influx of population into the southern part of the state and a more moderate one into the central part, coming from the northeast and midwest.

A great variety of bearers of traditional culture from other parts of the world, besides ancient and modern Indians, Spanish and Spanish-Americans, and English and Anglo-Americans, has come to Florida. Enslaved or free, *blacks* have always come with the Spanish and with the English; with Spanish-Americans and Anglo-Americans; from the Bahamas, Jamaica, and elsewhere. Generally, the blacks adopted the culture of those of European origin with whom they lived before coming to Florida, but preserving to some degree the base of their African culture and modifying and adapting the European culture to their own manner.

Other groups are too numerous to mention. Let us cite only three examples. Tarpon Springs won touristic fame for its *Greeks* who dived for sponges on the bottom of the Gulf of Mexico and for its spectacular pageantry on religious holidays in the Greek Orthodox church of Saint Nicholas. In 1885, a Russian immigrant built a railroad onto the Pinellas peninsula, and gave the name of his birthplace to a city: St. Petersburg, which gained world fame as a city of *oldsters,* who came from everywhere to pass their old age in a very agreeable climate. But they gave to the city a certain melancholic character which the city is trying to erase by supporting activities and practices typical of young people.

In 1927, the circus of Ringling Brothers and Barnum and Bailey decided to spend its winters in Sarasota, and *a great variety of people associated with a circus,* of different nationalities and closely united by their profession, established their residence there, and some have remained. I spent a night in that city with a group of Oriental students, among whom some from Thailand went out in search of food from their country. They soon found a fellow-countryman, owner of a small restaurant, where he served us a Thai banquet — in Sarasota! One would not expect to find the cultural mosaic the circus left in that little city.

Thus we see in Florida of the sixteenth and seventeenth centuries an indigenous culture and a Spanish culture that almost disappeared; a period of transition in the eighteenth century; and, since the nineteenth century, a culture basically Anglo-American, in its Southern form, still outstanding in the northern part of the state and clouded in the central and southern parts by an influx of very diverse elements—especially in the southeast where we find, notably, the Hispanic-American element, predominantly Cuban especially in Miami, and the Jewish element in Miami Beach.

This mosaic of traditional culture is so recent that its elements have not yet had time to adapt themselves to each other or to their new environment. So Florida lacks a well unified and rooted traditional culture. But in time it will be formed, because gradually its elements will adapt themselves to one another.

Examples of Traditional Culture

Let us cite some Indian, Hispanic, and Anglo-American examples. From such a vast store of culture, space here permits us to select only a few, drawn from observations of explorers, historians, and folklorists.

For the sixteenth century Indians, perhaps the best source is W. R. Jackson, Jr.'s, *Early Florida through Spanish Eyes*, University of Miami Hispanic American Studies, no. 12 (Coral Gables, 1954), which assembles what Spanish chroniclers of the sixteenth and seventeenth centuries say about the Indians, from the time Juan Ponce de León disembarked near the St. Augustine inlet in 1513 to the founding of St. Augustine by Pedro Menéndez de Avilés in 1565:

The Indians did not always receive the Spaniards with open arms. Indeed, when they understood that the Spaniards were looking for gold, jewels, or any riches in concentrated form that they could carry off to Spain, that they had legends of hidden treasures in Spain, and that the greedy tend to be credulous, the Indians told them legends, already known or invented on the spot, of fabulous riches in other places. Sometimes a guide would accompany them to show them such a place, and when the guide had them far enough away from his village that he thought they could not find their way back, he would disappear, leaving them lost.

Sometimes the Spanish themselves contributed to the legendary accounts of the Indians, as Elvas explains, because they feared that if they could not report on gold or silver or any other thing of value in Florida, it would acquire such a bad reputation that it would be difficult to get new recruits for the army. Elvas tells us that in the region of Paracoxi, to the north of Tampa, when the Spanish asked where they could find gold, the Indians told them that the people of Ocala fought with people of another region who, when they went to war, wore hats of gold as helmets.

More valuable than gold is youth, and the most popular legend was the

Mosiac of Traditional Culture

one about a fountain whose waters rejuvenated old people. Hernández de Oviedo tells us that in 1512 Ponce de León and his men suffered many woes searching for this fountain, which was a hoax of the Indians. In 1514, Pedro Mártir says that Alvarez de Castro as well as Luis Vásquez de Ayllón declare that they have heard of this fountain and believe somewhat in the legend, but have not seen it, because the inhabitants of Florida have sharp claws and defend their rights with great vigor. Nevertheless, he cites the case of an old man from the Bahamas who went to Florida, passed some time there drinking and bathing himself in the water of that fountain, and returned home rejuvenated and virile enough to marry again and have children. One asks: if nature permits the serpent to renew itself shedding its skin, why would she not allow man something similar?

Hernando Escalante Fontaneda says that Cuban Indians have bathed in every river, lake, and swamp of Florida and still go seeking that marvelous fountain. So it seems that many Indians believed that legand, found in world folklore since ancient times, and that some Spaniards took it seriously, while others made fun of it or remained doubtful but with the hope that it might be true. As a tourist attraction, a "Fountain of Youth" was established in St. Augustine.

Speaking of food, Fontaneda says that the Indians in southern Florida ate fish, sea turtles, snails, tuna, and whales. López de Velasco says that the Indians hunted the whale in the vicinity of Biscayne Bay, where Miami is now. José de Acosta says the Indians would come beside the whale in their canoe, drive sharp poles into the openings through which the whale breathed, and tie their canoe to the whale with a rope. Desperately the whale would rush here and there, and finally approach land and become stranded. On the beach they would kill it and cut it to pieces which they would dry and grind to convert the flesh into powder which would last them for a long time. Fontaneda says that there were turtles as large as a shield and had as much flesh as a cow.

Alvar Núñez Cabeza de Vaca, one of the most famous explorers, says that the Florida Indians could run from dawn to dusk pursuing a deer, until the animal would tire and they would kill it, although sometimes they would take it alive. One asks: why did they run so much when they could have killed the deer with an arrow? "The Inca," Garcilaso, tells us that one day the Spaniards removed the chains from an Indian of Apalache (the region of Tallahassee), gave him a bow and arrow and ordered him to shoot it from a distance of fifty paces at a coat of mail which they had placed over an Indian reed basket. The arrow passed through the coat of mail and the basket with so much force that if a man had been behind it, it would have passed through him too. They placed another coat of mail over the first one and the arrow passed through all.

For the modern Seminole Indians, let us use as sources the book of F. Densmore on Seminole music (Bureau of American Ethnology, Bulletin 161, 1956), which in its forty pages of introduction gives us a good survey of Seminole history, dwellings, dress, hunting, food, customs, beliefs, et cetera, and the book of L. Capron on the green corn dance (Bureau of American Ethnology, Bulletin 151, 1953).

Especially interesting are their beliefs and customs associated with death. They believe that sleep is a kind of temporary death, during which the spirit can leave the body. When it returns and the body awakes, one can remember his experiences outside of the body as dreams. When one dies, the spirit leaves the body not to return, even though it may remain near the body. The corpse is placed in a coffin, suspended on a long pole, and carried by men who chew bay leaves, which they believe will give them strength and will ward off evil spirits. They place the coffin in a canoe and take it deep within the swamp, where they leave it in a simple hut above the ground. Beside the coffin they place objects used in life (broken to release their ghosts) for the dead person's use, because it is believed that he continues his life more or less as before.

In mourning, the dead man's widow lets her hair down and removes her beads. Ritually, she is unclean, she must eat alone, and must not change clothes. In the next green corn dance, a widower strips off her old clothes for her and dresses her in new garments, and she is admitted again to normal life.

The green corn dance is the principal festival which the Seminoles celebrate every year in some isolated spot, far from intruders. During two or three days people are arriving, making their camps, preparing the dance circle, and setting up the post for the ball game of the boys and girls, who throw the ball to see who can hit a mark placed on the post at a height of some six feet.

At night there is dancing. Perforated tins attached to the calves of the women's legs, a kind of maracas, with beads, seeds, or pebbles inside, sharply mark the rhythm of the dance; those of the men produce a duller beat. Each man holds in his left hand a palmetto fan between his face and the fire. The dance director, seated to one side on a log, gives instructions for each dance and the words for the songs, and indicates when to start, change movement, and stop. Many dances are based on the actions of animals: the alligator, fox, owl, snake, and so forth. The dances usually continue for two or three hours.

When everyone has arrived and everything is in order, picnic day arrives. The medicine man distributes much beef among the camps, and during the whole day the people cook and eat until, at nightfall, the dances begin and last till midnight.

The following day is court day. At dawn, the medicine man and his helpers bathe, and he sings a petition that his magic may not harm him and that he can use it for the good of the Indians. His helpers prepare the first and second black drinks of medicinal herbs, in cold water. They blow prayers into the second black drink through a hollow reed. The men fast. At noon the court convenes, presided over by the old men. All the men and boys are present. The lesser faults of the past year are pardoned and the major ones are punished. He who enjoys the privilege of being a member of the group must respect its laws. Otherwise he is excluded from the group's ritual until he repents. If he persists in not repenting after having committed a serious crime, the group abandons him completely. Personal matters and general problems of the group are discussed. At nightfall, the medicine man's fire is lit. His medicine bundle of fetishes, amulets, et cetera, and the medicine bundles of various members of the camps are brought in. The third black drink of medicinal herbs is prepared in boiling water. It is left to boil until midnight, and then it is taken four times; but it must not be retained.

Meanwhile social dances have been danced. At midnight, the green corn dance is danced for the first time. This and other dances continue to be danced until dawn. With the fasting and the black drink, the men's bodies have been cleansed and purified. The sacred medicine, hidden during the rest of the year, has been brought out and is gathering power. The power of the medicine is maintained with song, dance, and ritual.

At dawn the women begin to prepare food: beef with rice and tomatoes, corn biscuits, and sofkee, a traditional Seminole drink. The skin of all the men and boys is scratched with needles, not enough to draw blood, but in order to purify it. A tarpaulin which covers two poles bent across each other in an arc forms a sweatbath, in which the men enter in groups and throw the black drink over heated stones. After a few moments in the steam, they emerge and go directly to bathe. The medicine man smokes his ceremonial pipe and inspects the medicine bundles, returns them to their owners, and hides his. When he returns, the green corn dance is ended and the feast begins.

The traditional culture which the Spanish brought to America, in spite of having developed many variations in the New World, has preserved quite well the unity of its character. Whether it be a *conquistador* of the seventeenth century, or an Ybor City tobacco worker of the nineteenth century, or a Cuban refugee in Miami of the twentieth century, who does not know some of the numerous traditional jokes and anecdotes of Quevedo, that seventeenth century Spanish author renowned for his wit and satire? The folk attribute many ancient tales to him. In my folktales collected in Ybor City *(Southern Folklore Quarterly,* 1938) I include one attributed to Quevedo and also to the Roman poet, Vergil, who became very popular in the Middle Ages. It says that he made love to two servant girls who lived on the third floor of the house where they worked. They promised to pull him up to their room in a basket with a rope at midnight. He appeared at the agreed hour, they lowered the basket, he got into it, they pulled him up halfway, tied the rope, and left him hanging. When the sun rose, all who passed through the street saw him and mocked him.

Josefina de la Grana gave me in Ybor City in 1936 the following rhyme which mothers use to entertain their babies while counting their fingers or toes:

> This poor little fellow was going along a little road
>   and he found a little egg.
> This one broke it.
> This one put salt on it.
> This one boiled it.
> And this shameless rascal
>   ate it.

It seems to me that this rhyme is based on a folktale known in Andalusia *(Folklore Andaluz,* 1883) about three poor brothers who had one boiled egg. They agreed that the one who could offer the most appropriate saying could eat the egg. The first one knocked it against the wall and said: *Casca cascorum.* (These brothers evidently think a saying in Latin is most impressive; this first one is an attempt to latinize Spanish *cáscara* [shell]. The second broke the shell more, put salt on it and said: *Sar, sale, sapiensa.* (These are based on Spanish *sal* [salt] and *sapiencia* [wisdom].) The third took off the shell, swallowed the egg, and said: *Consumatus est.*

Mosaic of Traditional Culture

(Latin *consummare*, Spanish *consumar* [to complete, finish]; also maybe with Latin *consumere* and Spanish *consumir* [to eat] in mind.) Here too we see the unity of traditional culture, from Andalusia to Florida.

The following verses will give the reader an idea of the Ybor City environment toward the end of the nineteenth century, with its mixture of Spanish and English together, with some words from the cigar makers' vocabulary. I was told they circulated from mouth to mouth as local folklore, though written in 1886 by a Tampa barber. I published them with the explanations they gave me *(Southern Folklore Quarterly,* 1937):

A este Quibués llegué yo [I reached this town of Key West],
cuando en La Habana embarqué [when I set out from Havana],
y al punto me enamoré [and at once I fell in love]
de una ledi de Nasó [with a lady from Nassau, a black girl].
Ella me dise, -Ay donó [She says to me, "I don't know (Spanish)"].
Tú espiqui tu mí cubano [You speak to me in Cuban (Spanish)"].
Pero con semblante ufano [But with a proud face],
hablando entre col y col [speaking diversely],
chapurreando el español [she hardly speaking any Spanish],
y yo hablando país y habano [and I speaking Havana dialect].
En el gueite la encontré [I met her at the gate],
y le dije, -?Yu laiqui mí? [and I said to her, "Do you like me?"].
-Yu plis comín hoy ["Please come in now"],
que me dijeron y entré [I was told and I went in].
-Serdan, yéntiman, fue ["Sit down, gentleman," was]
la segunda invitasión [the second invitation].
Le dije, -Escúsimi, olray [I said to her, "Excuse me, I'm all right];
escúsimi, ay an satisfay [excuse me, I'm satisfied"].
Y entré en la conversasión [And I entered into the conversation].
-?Buat yu buanti teli mí? ["What do you want to tell me?"].
Ay lobi plenti cubano ["I've loved plenty of Cubans].
Ay don laiqui americano [I don't like Americans],
mucho trompi quechi mí [I catch many blows, they treat me badly"].
Al punto la interrumpí [At once I interrupted her],
y le dije, -!Escrapiumáu! [and I said to her, "Shut your mouth!].
Yo quiero desirte nau [I want to tell you right now]
mí no laiqui faiti buit yu [I don't want to fight with you].
Mí cubano beri gut [I'm a very good Cuban],
y matrimonio enijáo [and matrimony anyhow, my intentions are serious].
No creas que esto es jonboc [Don't think this is humbug],
ni que vengo a coger raque [nor that I come to deceive you].
Tú verás que mí combaque [You'll see that I'll come back]
tumaro on seben ocloc [tomorrow at seven o'clock],
y aunque inglés mí no toc [and although I don't talk English],
mí com a desirte a ti [I come to tell you]

que el falla que tengo aquí [that the fire (of love) which I have here],
may dolin, sólo se quita [my darling, can only be extinguished]
besando yo esa boquita [by my kissing that little mouth]
que sólo bilón tu mí [that belongs only to me].
Ay an sigar mequen jía [I'm a cigar maker here],
beri suit doy a la bola [very sweet form I give to the cigars I make],
mí no buequi otra bitola [I don't work any other batch of cigars]
como no sea de regalía [except the best].
Ay gari moni, may día [I got money, my dear],
en el banco de Yon Juait [in the bank of John White],
y aunque ahora estamos de estraic [and though we're now on strike],
ay neba go tu dat plei [I never go to that place].
Si mí no buequi tudei [If I don't work today],
es porque a mí no me laic – [it's because I don't like (want) to"].

The blacks in Florida have adopted in great part the traditional culture of the whites with whom they have been associated — Spanish culture with the Spanish-Americans; English with the Anglo-Americans, adapting it to their norms; and also they have preserved something of their African culture, less among the Anglo-Americans, more among the Hispanic-Americans.

Notable among the Cuban blacks is what is described as *ñáñigo*, referring first to the individual associated with a secret society formed by blacks in Cuba and today a traditional culture expressed chiefly in music, songs, and dances of African origin. S. Kennedy *(Southern Folklore Quarterly,* 1940) describes an initiation dance on the street in Key West. First come three devils, sweeping the way for the initiates with brooms. Members of the society wear capes over their heads. One dancer beats the air with a stick to ward off evil spirits. Another comes with a goat and another with a rooster. Another has a porcupine in a cage and another has a snake on his arm. They lead the initiates into the water up to their waist. The one carrying the stick strikes the goat on the head, leaving it stunned, then pierces its throat with a knife. The initiates drink the blood. Then they dance on the beach. With yellow chalk an X is placed on their chest and head. They go to a nearby house, where the initiates kneel within a circle marked by chalk, and a ritual is performed with incantations in *ñáñigo,* a combination of Spanish and African dialects. Sometimes murders mysteriously occur during these initiation dances, and probably on this account they no longer are seen, at least openly, in Key West and Tampa.

C. H. Hauptmann *(Southern Folklore Quarterly,* 1939) gives a note on witchcraft in Tampa, brought chiefly by blacks from Cuba. In an inconspicuous section of Ybor City three corncobs hang on a door, indicating that this is a witchdoctor's house. Inside there is a table arranged somewhat like an altar, with crosses, incense, rosaries, and other objects associated with the Roman Catholic Church; and gourds, coconuts, flowers, and various gifts to Christian saints or African gods. Here the witchdoctor can produce an evil spell, called *salación* in Spanish. A spell becomes manifest in a mysterious ill, loss of sanity of a sweetheart, business failure, or any other misfortune that the witchdoctor can produce or against which he can effect a cure, called *limpieza* in Spanish, cleansing the *salación*. He may open a dead bird's breast and insert dried corn, seeds, buttons, nails, coins, fish-hooks, etcetera. Handed to and accepted by the intended victim, this medicine bundle will produce a *salación*.

For a woman who wishes to insure the fidelity of her husband, seven needles are inserted in a dove's heart with hairs from the husband wrapped around it, which she will bury in front of the house under a rue plant and her husband will be faithful as long as the rue plant flourishes. Sometimes the witchdoctors treat true bodily ills; but this would be practicing medicine without a license, which is against the law.

The traditional culture of the English survives in its typical American form, especially Southern, with the modifications and new creations produced by the new pioneer environment and by the mixture of various kinds of colonizers leveled in their harsh struggle in a land of undeveloped natural wealth, where they forged the typical American character. A good continuous source of data about Florida is the *Southern Folklore Quarterly,* a periodical published by the University of Florida in Gainesville since 1937.

In the half-dozen legends of Florida assembled by J. F. Doering *(Southern Folklore Quarterly,* 1938) we see that the legend in Florida, as in all other parts of the country, focuses its attention on the first inhabitants, Indians and pioneering Europeans, and on notable geographic features, about which the folk romantically weave fact with fiction. One says that Oklawaha, an Indian youth, and Winona, an Indian maiden, fell in love; but they could not marry because their tribes were enemies. One night, together in their accustomed place, they resolved that, if they could not be together in life, they would join in death, and they threw themselves into Silver Springs, where their bodies can still be seen on the bottom (land formations), eternally embraced.

In a more modern version, they are Anglo-Americans. Young Claire Douglass fell in love with Bernice Mayo, who was visiting her aunt in

Ocala, and he gave her a bracelet to seal their love pact. Claire's father, owner of a large plantation near Fort King, disapproving of this love affair, sent his son to Europe and intercepted his letters to Bernice. She believed that he had forgotten her and died of grief. He likewise believed that she had forgotten him. Finally he came home and, one day, when he was in a boat on the transparent waters of Silver Springs and looking down to its bottom, which could be seen very clearly despite its depth, he suddenly saw the corpse of his beloved Bernice, still wearing the bracelet he had given her, faithful till death. He threw himself into the water, embraced his sweetheart, and remained on the bottom with her forever.

About an Indian and Spanish girl we have the legend of Chichi-Okobee, a young Indian warrior, held as a hostage by Hernando de Soto, whose daughter Sara nursed him when he was ill, and they fell in love. Then she became ill and he brought a witchdoctor from his tribe to treat her; but she died. In his grief, Chichi-Okobee confessed to Hernando de Soto his love for his daughter and won the father's permission to select her burial site. For him, the most beautiful place in all Florida was the bay of Sarasota. Accompanied by other Indian warriors, Chichi-Okobee lowered the corpse of his beloved Sara into the bay, whereupon all slashed the bottoms of their canoes and drowned themselves, following her corpse to the bottom.

The "tall tale" enjoys the greatest popularity among Anglo-Americans. Let us cite a miscellany from *A Treasury of Southern Folklore* (1949), by B. A. Botkin, about hurricanes, climate, and topography.

They say that a hurricane wind blew with such force that it blew a well up out of the ground, straightened a crooked road, and scattered the days of the week so badly that Sunday did not appear until Tuesday morning. It stood up the ties of a railroad track so that it looked like a fence. It ripped various houses off their foundations, hurled them through the air, turned them around, and set them again on their foundations facing in the opposite direction from their previous position. They say that when the 1906 hurricane came, when Miami was a village just getting started, Judge Robert Taylor was playing pool. He stopped, ran to his office in the Fussell building where he met Judge George Worley on his knees praying, and he said to him, "Get up, George. You're not doing a bit of good. Let me try."

They say that, on Christmas Eve, God was going from St. Augustine to Palatka. It just happened that the Devil was going along the same road, in the opposite direction. God did not see him, because he was absorbed in

Mosaic of Traditional Culture

thought about how many presents he would have to buy for the new angels. But the Devil saw God, hid behind a stump, and jumped out when God passed by, shouting, *"Aguinaldo!"* (Spanish for "Christmas gift!"), to claim a Christmas gift. God said, "This is one time you caught me unaware." And looking back over his shoulder, God added, "Take the Atlantic coast. It is for this reason that the east coast of Florida has so many hurricanes—it belongs to the Devil."

The blessed climate of Florida with its sun that gives life to all is famed everywhere. They say that a young man gravely afflicted with tuberculosis was coming to Florida on a train, helped by a male nurse who had to carry him everywhere in his arms. The doctors had recommended to him that the sun treatment was his only hope. On arriving at Clearwater, a passenger on the train carelessly raised a window curtain and a ray of sun entered and fell directly upon the sick man. A second later the nurse heard a cry and saw his patient disappearing through the window. They went out in search of him; but he had not left the slightest trace. Two days later they found him in Sarasota in the Ringling Brothers circus, where they had hired him as a lion-tamer.

But sometimes that sun which gives life in Florida is a drawback for the natives of that healthful state. A Mr. Trussell of Miami, a seller of cemetery lots, said that his business was so bad that he was not selling anything, because nobody was dying in that salubrious climate. Finally, in order to demonstrate that the cemetery was still in business, they imported a corpse from Chicago and organized a solemn and impressive burial. Thousands came to witness the novelty. Beside the grave, they removed the coffin lid in order that the public might see this masterpiece of the undertaker's art, the manner of arranging the corpse so beautifully that it seemed to be alive. When that benign Florida sun smiled upon that body, the dead man, who had been a gunman, rose up with a shout looking for his pistol. They had to kill him again before they could go on with the burial.

A speech by Carl Dann of Orlando informs us about modifications of topography. He says that around 1860 his grandfather arrived in central Florida and saw that the land was completely flat, which did not please him, because it lacked hills like those of Pennsylvania where he was born. He knelt down and scraped up the dirt and sand and made the hills which are seen today in that region. On seeing what he was doing, Carl said to him, "Grandfather, don't take all the sand and dirt away from those people. You know that now there are many parts of Florida where you have to use a ladder to get up to the ocean." As water was lacking, his grandfather made all the lakes now seen in the central part of the state. It was a tremendous task, because he had to take up the water in gourds, bring it in an ox cart from the Atlantic coast, air it to get the salt out, and finally empty it in the great hollows he had scratched out.

He also made the St. Johns River; but like all famous people, he was bound to suffer the criticism of his neighbors. People said that since he was a Yankee from the North, he made the river run north and not south as a good Southerner would have done. Yankees enjoyed the reputation of having much pep, which it was believed the Southerners lacked. His grandfather, being a Yankee, began to dig out the St. Johns River bed near Jacksonville, wide and deep; but as he went progressing toward the south he kept losing his pep and dug out less and less until, on arriving below Orlando, he went to sleep.

If space permitted, beliefs and home remedies, customs and festivals could be described. I conclude citing only the title of the best collection of Florida ballads and songs: *Folksongs of Florida,* by A. C. Morris, who was professor of English at the University of Florida at Gainesville, where this work was published in 1950; and a stanza of one of the ballads in this work, about the hurricane that passed over Miami in 1928.

> God Almighty moved on the water
> and the peoples in Miami run.
> Some was floating on the ocean,
> and some was floating on the sea;
> and some was crying on bended knee,
> "Lord, have mercy on me."

Editor's Note: In 1976 the Seminoles gave their approval to an agreement with the U.S.A. government that will pay them sixteen million dollars for those 32,000,000 acres of land.

MEDICINE IN SPANISH FLORIDA
by William M. Straight, M.D.

Although the history of the United States as taught to my generation emphasized the Anglo-French beginnings on the North American continent, Florida has its beginnings in Spanish tradition. In this, the bicentennial year of our country, it seems fitting to recognize those hearty Spaniards who, oftentimes grimly, maintained a foothold in Florida for almost three hundred years. In the next several pages we will examine the history of Spanish Florida with particular attention to matters of health and disease, matters which importantly contributed to the grimness of life in the colony.

Don Pedro Menéndez de Avilés, the founder of St. Augustine, was dispatched from Spain in response to the French challenge of the Spanish title to *La Florida*. The French Huguenots had boldly constructed a fort on the south bank of the St. Johns River from which it was presumed they would prey on the Spanish treasure fleets that sailed along the east coast of Florida. Thus, upon landing (1565) near the site of the present-day Nombre de Dios Mission, Menéndez almost simultaneously began to build a fortification and dispatch parties to destroy the French at Fort Caroline and at Matanzas Inlet.[1]

The first shelter of the Menéndez expedition was a large dwelling at an Indian village on the site of the above mentioned mission. Later the Spaniards moved to Anastasia Island, and in 1570 they returned to the mainland and established themselves on the site of the present-day St. Augustine. Menéndez established a second fortified settlement, Santa Elena, on Port Royal Sound.

St. Augustine developed primarily as a military outpost and most of the inhabitants were soldiers with their wives and children, employees of the crown, slaves, and the clergy. It also served as a rescue station for mariners shipwrecked along the coast as far north as the present South Carolina.[2]

St. Augustine's town plan followed the decree of 1573 for towns in Spanish America. By 1586, a grid of four north-south streets and four east-west streets delineated nine city blocks located south of the present city plaza. To the north, the land was completely vacant until one reached the fort. The inhabitants lived in flimsy wooden houses with palmetto-thatched roofs. Initially there was no protecting wall about the city, but there was a wooden watchtower on Anastasia Island which was constantly manned to warn of an approaching enemy.[3] It was the sighting of this watchtower that led Sir Francis Drake to sack and burn St. Augustine in 1586. After that misfortune, the Spaniards began rebuilding immediately and concentrated their meager garrison in St. Augustine. Santa Elena was abandoned.[4]

By the turn of the seventeenth century, St. Augustine was still a primitive settlement of some 120 houses. The dirt streets became muddy whenever it rained and some were even flooded by high tides. Domestic animals roamed the streets freely.[5]

Gov. Gonzalo Mendez de Canzo improved St. Augustine during his administration (1597-1603). He established the plaza, a public market, weights and measures, a mill, and a hospital. He roofed the church with shingles and built a house for himself facing the plaza. This house was later purchased to serve as the governor's official residence. More important was his firm decision that the settlement would be maintained and would not be moved to Port Royal Sound as some advocated.[6]

Almost everyone in St. Augustine was in government employ in one capacity or another. Their clothing was imported from Mexico, either as the finished product (hats, breeches, and stockings—the latter, of English wool) or was made (coats, shirts, underwear) from yard goods also imported from Mexico. The diet of the people consisted of corn, beans, flour, pumpkin, lettuce, garlic, radishes, greens, peaches, pomegranates, and oranges. Meat was extremely scarce at first and usually imported; later it became somewhat more available as ranches developed in the rich back-country near present-day Tallahassee. Until then the chief protein came from fish, which could be had in abundance.[7]

St. Augustine was the base for the Franciscan friars who consolidated Spanish rule by converting the Indians to Christianity. In 1587, missions began dotting coastal Georgia and North Florida, and this was not halted by Indian revolts in 1597, 1647, and 1655. Accompanied by soldiers, the missionary conveyed the impression of power. This joint military and religious activity was a most natural procedure since Spanish royal authority comprised both secular and ecclesiastical jurisdictions.[8]

By 1668 England had become the chief rival of the Spanish in Florida. That year, pirate captain, John Davis (alias Robert Searles), sacked St. Augustine but could not take the wooden fort. Since he did not burn the city, the Spanish believed he would return to hold St. Augustine and use it as a base to raid shipping on the Spanish Main. This spurred the authorization in 1669 to build an adequate stone fortification. Another stimulus was the English settlement of Charleston in 1670, which lent credence to the Spanish suspicion of an English design against Florida.[9]

As the building of the present Castillo de San Marcos (1672-1696) neared completion, stone was made available for private construction in the city. The poverty of the people, however, prevented the widespread use of this material. Thus, in 1702 only sixteen houses were made of stone and one of these was the governor's residence. That year the English, led by Gov. James Moore of Carolina, besieged the Castillo unsuccessfully and upon withdrawal set St. Augustine afire.[10] The British also ravaged the missions across North Florida, destroying them during the early years of the eighteenth century.

St. Augustine was slow to rise from this destruction. By 1713 only the governor's residence had been reconstructed, and the common folk used straw and scorched boards to shelter themselves. New and permanent houses gradually appeared, so that by 1740 there were about 300 houses for the 2,062 people residing in the city. When the Spanish turned Florida over to the British in 1763, the population of St. Augustine numbered 3,000, and there were 124 stone, 140 tabby, and 78 wooden houses — a total of 342.[11]

The British soldiers destroyed the flimsier houses in St. Augustine to obtain scarce firewood, but the good buildings were improved with the addition of second stories, fireplaces, chimneys, and glazed windows. In 1784 when Florida reverted to Spain, 110 of some 277 houses were considered uninhabitable.[12]

A count in 1788 yielded 1,000 residents and 114 stone, 19 tabby, and

133 wooden houses in the city, a total of 266. About 100 wooden structures were mere shacks, the products of the hectic loyalist migration from the rebellious colonies during the previous decade.[13]

When Spain ceded Florida to the United States in 1821, the population of St. Augustine numbered 2,000 and the houses 300. There were also 2,000 persons living on plantations in the countryside. About one half of the population were slaves.[14]

When Menéndez landed in September 1565, he brought with him two surgeons, five barbers, and an apothecary with "a box containing medicine for the curing of the sick."[15] However, as was the custom in those days, these initial medical men soon returned to the old country and St. Augustine was to be without a physician or surgeon for periods of time in the succeeding centuries. Thus, in July 1582, Gov. Pedro Menéndez Marqués wrote to the King that he had been ill for nine months, having become paralyzed from going into the swamps and woods after the Indians of Guale (an area of coastal Georgia, particularly St. Catherines Island) and Santa Elena, and that since there was no physician or medicine in the colony, he feared he would not be cured "if the illness ripens."[16]

As we have seen, the restless sea that pounded the sandy coast was a chief source of food, but at times it brought other benefits. Indeed, the first physician to remain with the colony for a considerable length of time, Juan de LeConte, was cast on the beach at Santa Elena when his ship, *El Príncipe,* was driven ashore in a storm about 1579.

At first, LeConte was a prisoner, serving as physician, surgeon, and barber in return for his lodging, relations, and clothing. In 1586, he was officially allowed to occupy the position of surgeon in the Florida garrison with a salary of four ducats monthly. In 1602, having served "more than 23 years" he approached the Governor for permission to return to Spain or an increase in pay to forty ducats as he was "old and tired and cannot support himself with the four ducats he received every month and the ration of an ordinary private." The Governor, being unable to increase his salary and unwilling to permit his only physician-surgeon to leave the colony, encouraged him to petition the King directly and wrote a commendatory letter to the King on his behalf. In the letter the Governor notes that he had a "wide knowledge in the art of medicine," and that "if God, our Lord, had not sent him to this garrison, men would die as animals." It is further noted that he cared for the soldiers, slaves, laborers, women, and children. The Governor stated, "A more competent person could not be secured for a thousand ducats."[17] Having read the letter from the Gover-

Medicine in Spanish Florida

nor to the King, LeConte increased his salary request by ten fold. In 1603, the Crown authorized the Governor to increase LeConte's salary—not ten fold as requested by the surgeon, but only to ten ducats.[18]

At other times in the history of St. Augustine, the populace had to depend upon physicians and surgeons of doubtful value. Thus, on April 30, 1685, Governor Cabrera writing to the Crown states, "When I took possession of this governorship in 1680 the only physician or surgeon here was Carlos Robson, of English nationality, who held the position of *cirujano mayor* (chief surgeon) and who had been baptized in this garrison. Not only is he not a physician or a qualified surgeon, but also he is deprived of consciousness most of the time by being drunk."[19] Again, in August of 1739, another governor writes to his superior in Havana, "Although we have also great need for a physician, if there is not a competent one to be found, we will manage with the *cirujano* of the garrison who, were he not so taken by *aguardiente* [rum], is not bad, but everybody refrains from calling him."[20] This same governor two years prior had written his superior in Cuba urging him to coerce a physician (*médico*) to come to St. Augustine, pointing out that previous efforts had been unrewarding. He goes on to state, "Although I consider that there will not be a man of average intelligence who will consent coming here, unless Your Lordship works his authority toward this end."[21] Twenty years later, a parish priest writing to the secretary of state for the Indies declares, "No less harmful is the damage experienced by the lack in this garrison of a skilled physician or surgeon, seemingly an irremediable and most harmful omission for these poor dwellers, due either to the unwillingness of individuals educated in this profession or to the limited salaries assigned to them, that they do not overcome the horror that the mention of Florida causes in everyone."[22]

Not only were the inhabitants of St. Augustine injured by the incompetence or drunkenness of their surgeons, but also on at least one occasion a surgeon incited a pirate attack on the city. In 1668, Gov. Francisco de la Guerra y de la Vega, "instigated by feminine gossip and meddling, treated the French surgeon of the garrison, Pedro Piques, badly and even slapped him." He then discharged him and refused to give him 200 pesos in accrued pay for his services during the previous two years. The governor put him on a ship bound for Havana. The ship was captured by the English pirate, John Davis, to whom Piques, thirsting for revenge, revealed the condition of St. Augustine's defenses, prompting the pirate to descend on the city at 1:00 a.m. on May 29, 1668. The pirates swarmed through the streets, catching the residents asleep. Hearing the commotion, the residents emerged from their houses and some were shot or knifed to death as they fled to the protection of the woods. The pirates, however, were repulsed in their assault on the fort. With the advent of daylight, the pirates systematically looted the homes and churches and boarded a ship in the harbor. On June fifth they sailed away.[23]

Another medical man who indirectly added to the troubles of St. Augustine was Dr. Henry Woodward. This young "chirurgeon" from North Carolina had gone to live with the Indians at Santa Elena and there was captured by the Spanish and taken to St. Augustine. In St. Augustine as a "willing prisoner" he lived with the parish priest, professed Catholicism and served as surgeon for the presidio. He escaped with John Davis during the same raid and later returned to Charleston, South Carolina, where he was highly influential in inducing the uncommitted Indians to withhold their allegiance from the Spaniards.[24]

In addition to physicians and surgeons, the medical needs of the people were met by barbers, apothecaries, nurses, and midwives. For example, at the muster of the Florida garrison in St. Augustine in 1578, "There was present Hernando de Segovia, barber, a native of Mérida, who appeared with his sword, buckler and case of instruments for making cures."[25] Apothecaries were always present in the colony, but at times there were no drugs available, as in November 1674.[26] As early as 1537 the Spanish king had put out an order that the physician could not dispense his own medication, for this was the province of the apothecary.[27] A ruling of the Crown also provided for a deduction from the soldier's pay to cover the cost of drugs and medicines he might require. Although the drugs were usually furnished by the Crown, apparently at times they were obtainable from other sources. In June of 1813 a resident of St. Augustine requested permission to sell certain medicaments such as camphor, alum, cream of tartar, manna, cathartic salt, and jallap which he had in his possession and which were scarce in the town.[28]

The nursing of the sick was carried out by convicts or by a soldier who served as nurse for the hospital and sexton for the hermitage of La Soledad, to which the hospital was initially attached. At times, a slave was assigned to make the beds, cook for the patients, and keep the hospital clean. The first such "housekeeper" of record was a royal slave, Maria Joijo.[29]

Midwives are mentioned in St. Augustine first on April 8, 1744,[30] and the note is made that they were permitted to administer baptism if the need

Medicine in Spanish Florida

were urgent and a priest not immediately available. The names of a number of midwives appear in the registry of baptisms of Saint Augustine Parish. As we have previously noted, the doctors of St. Augustine cared for women, but it is not known whether they performed deliveries.

As early as 1541, Emperor Don Carlos (Charles I) issued an order that in all Spanish and all Indian villages under the control of Spain, hospitals were to be opened where the sick poor could obtain medical attention. This edict was followed in 1573 by another put forth by his son, Phillip II, that hospitals for poor and noncontagious patients were to be built near the churches and managed by the Church, and another hospital for contagious diseases was to be built away from the village in the highest place.[31]

Prior to the advent of the official hospital in St. Augustine, the sister of Gov. Pedro Menéndez Marqués, Doña Catalina Menéndez, cared for the ill soldiers in her home and "spent from her estate in providing treatment to ill soldiers."[32]

The first record we have of a hospital in St. Augustine is in a letter from Gov. Gonzalo Méndez de Canzo to the Crown, dated February 23, 1598, in which he states that when he arrived in 1597 a hospital was being established in conjunction with the Hermita de Nuestra Señora de La Soledad (Church of Our Lady of Solitude). Canzo states that, had the hospital not been in operation during the summer of 1597, many soldiers, Indians, and black royal slaves would have died of the epidemic fever. He then tells the Crown that the cost of founding the hospital had exceeded the amount of contributions by more than 500 ducats (a familiar story even in this day), and he petitioned the Crown for financial support and for the assignment of a female black royal slave to make the beds, cook for the patients, and keep the place clean. To cover the cost of operation, the King was asked to supply 500 ducats annually.[33] There is little description of this hospital, but it is presumed that it was of thatch construction and that the beds consisted of pallets on the floor (wooden bedsteads were introduced in the eighteenth century).

This, the first hospital within the present limits of the continental United States, served until 1599 when a fire destroyed the Franciscan convent and it became necessary to house the missionary priests in the Church of Our Lady of Solitude, where the hospital was located.[34]

There now being no place where the sick soldiers and citizenry could be cared for, in January 1600, Governor Canzo "Founded at my expense a house of boards for use as a hospital... with its rooms in the attic and having beds with their mattresses, blankets, sheets, and pillows for the stated purpose that all poor and sick people may seek shelter by going to it." This palmetto-thatched hospital of six beds (so arranged about an altar in the center of the room that the patients might attend mass without leaving their beds) was dedicated to "the Lady Santa Bárbara." To cover the cost of operation of the hospital, the King supplied 500 ducats annually, and each soldier had deducted from his pay 12 reales annually; the 2½ reales daily stipend of the soldier was turned over to the hospital for each day spent in confinement. In addition to this, alms were solicited and farmers were requested to donate foodstuffs. The physicians and surgeons of the garrison were instructed to attend the patients, and the medicines were provided by the king.[35]

In 1605, the Franciscan convent having been rebuilt and the Church of Our Lady of Solitude having been repaired, enlarged, and freed from the danger of fire, Gov. Pedro de Ibarra, Canzo's successor, moved the hospital of Santa Bárbara and the patients back to the original hospital. He also had some unpleasant things to say about the location of the Santa Bárbara Hospital. He stated that of six patients who had been there three had died and the other three would never recover due to the unhealthy site chosen by Canzo.[36]

In 1657 there were apparently two hospitals in operation to care for the 300 Spanish residents and an unstated number of Indians. These are described as "a royal hospital dedicated to Nuestra Señora de la Soledad, ...another hospital for curing the poor who are sick,..."[37] The pirate John Davis (1668) sacked the hospital and, shortly after his attack, the Governor sent an urgent request to Mexico for quantities of cloth for sheets and mattresses and other small items for the hospital.[38]

In May of 1682, Governor Cabrera, feeling that the parish of Saint Augustine had not managed the hospital well, decided to ask the Order of San Juan de Dios[39] to take over the administration of the royal hospital. This led to conflicts with the parish and the Franciscans, both of whom feared that more priests would move in to share the meager alms. Being unable to resolve the conflict, Cabrera provided that a hospital be built on another site which would be supported with a share of his income and with the deductions from the soldiers. This left the parish with a hospital but no revenues. Until the new hospital was opened, the priests of San Juan de Dios would serve as both surgeons and apothecaries proceeding in the manner as previous surgeons and apothecaries had proceeded. The temporary arrangement seems to have provided for the surgeon and

Medicine in Spanish Florida

apothecary to prescribe treatment outside the hospital for sick soldiers, which treatment would be administered in the hospital in the Church of Our Lady of Solitude by the parish-controlled nurse.[40]

In the siege of 1702, the forces of Gov. James Moore of South Carolina burned all of St. Augustine except the Church of Our Lady of Solitude, the adjacent hospital, and some twenty houses.[41] In the years that followed, the hospital continued to be supported by deductions from the salary of the garrison and even one peso monthly from the meager remuneration given to convicts and slaves for their work.

The parish priest, Juan José Solana, describes the St. Augustine hospital in April of 1759 as the "newly rebuilt" former residence of Francisco Menéndez Marqués, deceased accountant of Florida. He states, "It has two large rooms, one on the ground level, the other upstairs, each with a capacity of twelve beds. There are two interior rooms downstairs, reserved for elderly persons. There is a masonry kitchen roofed with boards. In a room in the kitchen live two convicts who care for the sick. The hospital has a lot so spacious that medicinal herbs could be planted in it." In the same letter Solana gives us an insight into the operation of the hospital. He states, "The almost complete destitution experienced by the poor patients deserves no little attention from the pious concern of Your Most Illustrious Lordship [Bishop of Cuba]. This hospital receives every month 500 reales deducted from the soldiers, and one real a day from the hospitalized patients. Yet due to the lack of an individual employed exclusively to take care of the patients there is experienced so much carelessness in temporal and spiritual matters that it would cause compassion in the least compassionate heart and even in the most tyrannical. I propose that the governor and the Bishop, or his vicar, elect a majordomo who has demonstrated inclination toward compassion, with a salary equivalent to that of a gunner, a lieutenant, and a fusilier combined, and that one, two, or as many convicts as necessary, be subject to the majordomo to attend to the urgencies and needs of the patients."[42]

In the remainder of this chapter we will discuss the various illnesses recorded as occurring in St. Augustine and some of the therapies used. Seldom in the archival material thus far studied is there mention of specific remedies; therefore we will cite from the writings of the contemporary physicians, Monardes and Francisco Hernández, treatments used during this period.

The accounts of Florida in the sixteenth and seventeenth centuries glow in the best Chamber of Commerce tradition. Thus a geography book of 1688 states: "The area of Florida and Carolina is so temperate that men live to the age of 250 years, while the children of five generations are all alive at the same time."[43]

Earlier we have mentioned the first specific illness noted, the paralysis suffered by Gov. Pedro Menéndez Marqués. He stated at that time that he had been paralyzed for the previous nine months but was gradually recovering. The next specifically recorded instance of illness was Gov. Domingo Martínez who, when returning from an inspection trip, began to vomit blood and, on November 24, 1595, apparently died of a hemorrhage from the stomach.[44]

Chills and fever are frequently noted but it is not possible to diagnose the causative illness. Ashburn, a student of epidemic diseases,[45] believes there was no malaria among the Huguenots or the Spanish in the early days of settlement, but that malaria came later with the introduction of slaves. The first mention of quinine appears in a religious book which was published in Spain in 1639 and written by an Augustinian monk by the name of Calancha. We have found no record of quinine being used at St. Augustine during the first or second Spanish period.

A severe epidemic of smallpox was present in the town in 1655. Gov. Diego de Rebolledo notes that it had been present for ten months, the Indians and inhabitants had suffered greatly, and that work on the fort was at a standstill.[46] Still other epidemics of smallpox are recorded.[47] We have thus far discovered no evidence that inoculation was used in St. Augustine to fight this disease. On November 10, 1803, the king of Spain dispatched an expedition to bring smallpox vaccination to the new world. In order that they would have fresh vaccine on their arrival, they brought along twenty-two children whom they inoculated at intervals during the trip.[48] There is no record that this expedition visited St. Augustine.

As in other colonial areas, epidemic measles was at least once a highly fatal disease in Spanish Florida. Thus, in 1659, epidemic measles killed 10,000 Indians and many soldiers of the garrison at St. Augustine.[49]

There are many reports of syphilis *(gálico),* and on one occasion this disease incapacitated the mason in charge of the work at Castillo de San Marcos.[50] The specific remedy for this disease according to Monardes was the "holie woodde" now known as guaiacum, a tree found in tropical America. Monardes tells us about the discovery of this medicine: "A Spanyarde that did suffer greate paines of the Poxe, which he had by the companie of an indian woman, but his servaunte beyng one of the phisitions of that countrie, gave unto hym the water of Guaiacan, wherewith not only his greevous paines were taken awaie, that he did suffer, but healed verie well of the evill, and moste certainlie ... it healeth moste perfectly, without turnyng to fall againe, except the sicke man doe returne to tumble in the same bosome, where he tooke the firste."[51]

Because of a custom of continuing a man after he was crippled or ill as a member of the garrison on a "dead pay" status, we have, from time to time, lists of soldiers specifying their disabilities. A review of these lists reveals such diagnoses as "absolutely blind and deaf; old and habitually ill; habitually indisposed; asthmatic; disuse of a limb due to disease or accident; bent or crooked due to an accident; blind and demented; blind and ruptured; hobbled and ruptured; gouty; palsied [paralysis with a tremor]; leg broken by gun shot; paralyzed and short sighted due to organic defect." In the case of an 83-year-old Capt. Sebastian Lopez de Toledo, the diagnosis is "very exhausted" (*"muy postrado"*).[52] In some instances the diagnosis is easily recognized, as in the case of Sublieutenant Luis García de Mena who was "threatened by tisis [pulmonary tuberculosis], the beginning of which is indicated by the blood which he spits when he coughts."[53] On another occasion we are told, "When he dropped anchor in this port *Patrón* [Skipper] Matamoros experienced his last hardship, a *sofocación* [suffocation] which followed the labored respiration from which he was suffering, so sudden that he did not have time to receive any sacraments."[54] Possibly this was acute pulmonary edema due to congestive heart failure.

The wonder drug of the day was sassafras, which was found in Florida. We are told that it was given to the Huguenots at Fort Caroline by the Indians and the knowledge of it conveyed to the Spanish by survivors of the Huguenot massacre. Gonzáles Barcia tells us it was brought to Seville in 1567. He states that it was a sovereign remedy against "killing oppilation." It also was soothing to the liver and stomach; it would take away the tertian ague and cause long fevers to desist, restored the appetite, cured headaches, chest aches and pains in the side; it caused stones to be passed, induced micturation and menstruation; it cured paralysis, relieved the toothache, cured gout quickly, and made the hands benumbed by illness agile. It also soothed the abdomen and relieved motherhood sickness. It promoted fecundity, preserved from plagues, and was most useful in all cold humors, protracted illnesses, and flatulence.[55] Monardes adds that it was useful in "any maner of Reumes or Runnynges or Windinesse...."[56]

Another remedy to be found in Florida was tobacco. This was useful for many things including headaches, shortness of breath, and the treatment of chronic ulcers. The cough and expectoration produced by the tobacco smoke was thought to clear out the lungs and thus help shortness of breath. This remedy, it is said, was learned from the Indians and, indeed, LeMoyne, the Huguenot artist, in one of his drawings shows the Indians inhaling tobacco smoke.[57] Monardes also states that it is very useful for the treatment of "olde rotten soares although thei bee cankered." He advises, "Let the sicke man bee pourged with the counsaill of a phisition, and let hym bloud if it bee needful and then take this herbe and piunde it in a Morter, and take out the joice and put it into the Soare, and then after the maner of a Plaister put the stamped leaves upon it... and this doe once every daie, eatyng good meates, and not exceedyng in any disorder for otherwise it will not profite."[58]

Thus far we have uncovered very little specific information about the practice of surgery in St. Augustine. LeConte, the French barber surgeon who served the colony from about 1579 to about 1630, was certified by the sergeant major of Florida as skillful in "curing effectively all kinds of diseases and wounds...from arrows, pikes, halberds, and arquebuses, and broken legs, arms and heads."[59]

In a battle between the Spanish and the Indians on September 3, 1705, Ens. Francisco Ponce de León was shot in the arm, shattering the bone. It was necessary to amputate the arm, but immediately after the amputation Don Francisco died.[60]

In September 1727, Juan Frisonou, chief surgeon of the Florida garrison, certifies that the governor, Don Antonio de Benavides, had developed "an abscess which has appeared between the two cheeks which fall from the lower part of the coccyx, from which he has acquired some impediment in urinating, some continuous evacuations, fever, and other troubles ...." The surgeon further states that the Governor "cannot be cured in this said garrison for the total lack of medicaments and the necessary instruments."[61]

The Governor went to Havana where the physician and surgeon, Carlos del Rey, "found him with a great inflammation in the rectum with a fistula in the rectum four *dedos* deep (72 millimeters), originated from an abscess, which illness was accompanied by other illnesses [such as] obstructions in the glands of the mesentery;...the operation on said fistula was performed on him, opening it from the beginning to the end."[62]

Finally, we have uncovered one instance in which the history of St.

Augustine may have been changed by the advent of disease. In 1680, Sgt. Maj. Juan Márquez Cabrera, about whom we have spoken before, became governor. Cabrera was apparently a testy character with a facility for alienating people. This personality trait was aggravated by an illness which is described by a Dr. Francisco Moreno de Alba as "some arthritic pains complicated with a trace of *gálico* (syphilis). The pains are felt in his soft and spermatic parts, which are naturally cold, and a paralytic affection is beginning in the nerves and ligaments, threatening the deadening of a leg, which has a mature and inflamed chronic cutaneous infection, resulting from crusty, well-developed carbuncles, and from his extreme weakness."[63]

In the several years that Cabrera had been governor he had succeeded in alienating the soldiers and officers of the garrison, the Indians, the citizens of the town, and the clergy. During the Holy Week of 1687 he went to one of the priests for his annual confession. The priest refused to confess him as did other priests whom he consulted. He boarded a ship ready to sail for Havana, ostensibly to inspect the ship but actually intending to go to that city to find a priest who would confess him. As it was considered near treason for a governor to leave his province without the permission of the King, the Royal Treasurer, who had gone aboard the ship with the Governor, exhorted him to change his mind and return to shore. The Treasurer pointed out that the colony would be without a governor and, indeed, St. Augustine was direly in need of a governor. He also pointed out that the King and Queen would not look favorably upon this breach of his responsibilities. In a fit of anger, the Governor, it was quoted, replied, "S——t on St. Augustine; the King and Queen can go to hell."[64] Perhaps had he not been ill, in addition to having a testy personality, Governor Cabrera would have continued as governor of Florida and the course of history would have been different.

Acknowledgments

The search and translation of the Spanish documents, which are the major source of the information herein presented, was performed by Mr. Luis R. Arana of St. Augustine, and supported by U.S. Public Health Service Grant No. 1-RO1 — LM-00074-01, awarded to the University of Miami, Coral Gables, Florida. Mr. Arana was born in Puerto Rico.

Growth of St. Augustine During the Spanish Period

Year	Total Population	Number of Houses	Reference
1598	625	120	5
(Present Castillo de San Marcos built 1672-1696)			
1689	1,444	——	10
1702	1,500	172	10
1740	2,062	300	11
1763	3,000	342	11
(Florida belonged to Britain 1763-1784)			
1788	1,000	266	13
1821	2,000	300	14
(Florida belonged to the United States after 1821)			

NOTES

[1] Woodbury Lowery, *The Spanish Settlements Within the Present Limits of the United States: Florida, 1562-1574* (New York, 1905), pp. 103, 108, 158, 168-177, 189-199.

[2] Verne E. Chatelain, *The Defenses of Spanish Florida, 1565-1763* (Washington, 1941), pp. 15, 21, 44, 46-47; Charles W. Arnade, *Florida on Trial: 1593-1602* (Miami, 1959), pp. 77-78.

[3] Chatelain, *The Defenses*, pp. 30, 129 note 4; the Boazio map of St. Augustine and key in Julian S. Corbett, *Drake and the Tudor Navy*, 2 vols. (London, 1912), 2: 56.

[4] Chatelain, *The Defenses*, pp. 50, 51.

[5] Arnade, *Florida on Trial*, pp. 8, 9.

[6] Arnade, *Florida on Trial*, pp. 8, 9, 90; Gov. Pedro de Ibarra of Florida to the Crown, St. Augustine, Jan. 8, 1604, Archivo General de Indias (*hereafter* AGI) 54-5-9/47, Stetson Collection (*hereafter* SC).

[7] Arnade, *Florida on Trial*, p. 9; Charles W. Arnade, "Cattle Raising in Spanish Florida, 1513-1763," *Agricultural History* 35, No. 3 (July 1961); the royal officials of Florida to the Crown, Florida, Sept. 14, 1713, fol. 4, AGI 58-2-3/58, SC.

[8] Michael V. Gannon, *The Cross in the Sand: The Early Catholic Church in Florida, 1513-1870* (Gainesville, 1965), pp. 38-43, 47, 54, 56-58, 61-64; C. H. Haring, *The Spanish Empire in America* (New York, 1947), pp. 179-182.

[9] Chatelain, *The Defenses*, pp. 62, 151 note 18.

[10] Albert C. Manucy, *The Building of Castillo de San Marcos* (Washington, 1942); Charles W. Arnade, *The Siege of St. Augustine in 1702* (Gainesville, 1959); Mark F. Boyd, Hale G. Smith, and John W. Griffin, *Here They Once Stood: The Tragic End of the Apalachee Missions* (Gainesville, 1951); Gov. Diego de Quiroga y Losada of Florida to the Crown, St. Augustine, June 8, 1690, AGI 54-5-12/102, SC; Gov. Francisco de Corcoles y Martínez of Florida to the Crown, St. Augustine, Aug. 13, 1709, AGI 58-1-28/66, SC.

[11] Albert Manucy, *The Houses of St. Augustine: Notes on the Architecture from 1565 to 1821* (St. Augustine: The Historical Society, 1962), pp. 25-28, 33; Gov. Manuel de Montiano of Florida to Gov. Juan Francisco de Güemes of Havana, St. Augustine, May 9, 1740, East Florida Papers (*hereafter* EFP), series 37, letter No. 197.

[12] Manucy, *The Houses*, pp. 34, 35, 38-39, 41.

[13] Manucy, *The Houses*, pp. 43, 46.

[14] Manucy, *The Houses*, pp. 10, 45.

[15] Eugenio Ruidiaz y Caravia, *La Florida, su Conquista y Colonización por Pedro Menendez de Avilés*, 2 vols. (Madrid, 1893), 2: 558, 560, 565.

[16] Gov. Pedro Menéndez Marqués of Florida to the Crown, St. Augustine, July 6, 1582, fol. 2, AGI 54-5-16/27, SC.

[17] Master Juan de Laconte to the Crown, St. Augustine, May 4, 1611, fols. 4, 5, 12, 14, AGI 54-5-17/68, SC; Gov. Gonzalo Méndez de Canzo of Florida to the Crown, St. Augustine, May 22, 1602, fol. 2, AGI 54-5-9, Woodbury Lowery, Florida Manuscript (*hereafter* WL), vol. 4.

[18] Crown to the governor of Florida, Valladolid, March 22, 1603, fols. 278-278v, AGI 86-5-19 (SD 2528), SC.

[19] Gov. Juan Márquez Cabrera of Florida to the Crown, St. Augustine, April 30, 1685, fol. 1, AGI 54-5-15/17, SC.

[20] EFP, series 37, letter No. 154, Gov. Manuel de Montiano of Florida to Gov. Juan Francisco de Güemes of Havana, Florida, Aug. 16, 1739, fol. 178.

[21] Montiano to Güemes, Feb. 15, 1738, fol. 63v, EFP, series 37, letter No. 24.

[22] Parish priest Juan José Solana of St. Augustine to the secretary of state for the Indies, Julián de Arriaga, St. Augustine, April 9, 1760, fol. 33, AGI 86-7-21/41, SC.

[23] Sgt. Maj. Nicholas Ponce de León of Florida to the Crown, St. Augustine, Aug. 6, 1668, AGI 54-5-18/73, North Carolina Collection (*hereafter* NC) 682; Accountant Juan Menéndez Marqués of Florida to the Crown, Florida, July 4, 1668, AGI 54-5-18/70, SC.

[24] "Medical Men and Medical Events in Early St. Augustine," *J. Florida M.A.* 39 (August 1952): 116.

[25] Jeanette T. Connor, *Colonial Records of Spanish Florida*, 2 vols. (DeLand, 1925, 1930), 2: 137.

[26] Capt. Francisco de Reina of Florida to the Crown, St. Augustine, Nov. 17, 1676, fol. 1, AGI 54-5-19/19, SC.

[27] Francisco Guerra, *Historiografía de la Medicina Colonial Hispanoamericana* (Mexico, 1953) p. 32.

[28] Cabildo Records, fol. 51, EFP, series 412.

[29] Ens. Bartolomé Lopéz Gavira to the Governor of Florida, St. Augustine, Sept. 12, 1600, fol. 3, AGI 54-5-16/106, SC; AGI 54-5-15/17, fol. 1, SC; AGI 86-7-21/41, fol. 34, SC.

[30] St. Augustine Parish Registers: Group IV, Baptisms 1735-1763.

[31] Guerra, *Historiografía*, p. 30.

[32] Council of the Indies to the Crown, Madrid, Nov. 3, 1629, fol. 1, AGI 53-1-6/42, SC.

[92] THE HISPANIC PRESENCE IN FLORIDA

[33] Gov. Gonzalo Méndez de Canzo of Florida to the Crown, St. Augustine, Feb. 23, 1598, fols. 10-11, AGI 54-5-9, WL 4; Council of the Indies to the Crown, Madrid, Aug. 16, 1598, fol. 4, AGI 53-1-6/8, SC.

[34] Gov. Gonzalo Méndez de Canzo of Florida to the Crown, St. Augustine, Feb. 28, 1600, fol. 1v, AGI 54-5-9/32, SC.

[35] Gov. Pedro de Ibarra of Florida to the Crown, St. Augustine, Dec. 26, 1605, fol. 6, AGI 54-5-9/64, SC; AGI 54-5-9/32, SC; AGI 54-5-15/17, fols. 17-23, SC.

[36] AGI 54-5-9/64, fols. 5-6, SC.

[37] Juan Díez de la Calle, *Noticias Sacras y Reales de los Dos Imperios de las Indias Occidentales de la Nueva España*, 2 vols. (1659), fol. 4, WL 8.

[38] Marqués de Mancera, viceroy of New Spain, to the Crown, Mexico, April 20, 1669, fols. 50, 73, AGI 58-2-2/14, NC.

[39] The Order of San Juan de Dios was founded in Granada in 1540. Initially, its members provided for the care of the sick poor, but during the seventeenth and eighteenth centuries they became the medical corps of the Spanish armies and were appointed to administer hospitals throughout Spain and Spanish America. At the close of the eighteenth century, they numbered 2,915 *religiosi* serving in 281 hospitals (*Spanish Influence on Progress of Medical Science* [London: Welcome Foundation, 1935], p. 43). Members of this order served as physicians, surgeons, apothecaries and nurses (Francisco Barado, *Museo Militar: Historia del ejército español*, 3 vols. [Barcelona, c. 1883], 3: 578).

[40] AGI 54-5-15/17, fols. 6-9, 25-26, 30-38, 45-49, 50-59, SC.

[41] Arnade, *The Siege*, p. 57; The Tribunal of Accounts in Cuba to the Crown, Havana, Jan. 10-14, 1752, fols. 154-155.

[42] AGI 86-7-21/41, fols. 34, 35, SC.

[43] Morden, *Geography Rectified, or a Description of the World*, (London, 1688), p. 588.

[44] Factor Alonso de las Alas of Florida to the Crown, St. Augustine, Jan. 11, 1596, fols. 1, 2-3, AGI 54-5-16, WL3.

[45] P.M. Ashburn, *Ranks of Death: A Medical History of the Conquest of America* (New York, 1947), p. 117.

[46] Gov. Diego de Rebolledo of Florida to the Crown, St. Augustine, Oct. 24, 1655, fol. 1, AGI 58-2-2/2, SC.

[47] In 1732, 1740, 1758, and 1814.

[48] Arturo P. Prats, "Contribution of Spanish Physicians to the Culture and Colonization Effort of Spain in America," *Annals Royal National Academy of Medicine 82* (1965), pp. 327-352.

[49] Gov. Alonso de Aranguiz y Cotes of Florida to the Crown, St. Augustine, Nov. 1, 1659, fol. 2, AGI 58-2-2/4, SC.

[50] Montiano to Güemes, Aug. 8, 1738, fols. 107v-108, EFP, series 37, letter No. 74.

[51] Nicholas Monardes, *Joyfull Newes Out of the Newe Founde Worlde*, 2 vols. (Sevilla, 1574), trans. John Frampton (1577; reprint ed., London: Constable and Co., Ltd., 1925), p. 28.

[52] Gov. Manuel de Montiano of Florida to the secretary of state for the Indies, Marqués de la Ensenada, St. Augustine, Jan. 21, 1745, fol. 33, AGI 87-3-12/70, SC.

[53] Montiano to Güemes, Aug. 30, 1740, fol. 302, EFP, series 37, letter No. 221.
[54] Montiano to Güemes, Jan. 31, 1741, fol. 336v, EFP, series 37, letter No. 255.
[55] Andrés González Barcia, *Chronological History of the Continent of Florida*, trans. Anthony Kerrigan (Gainesville, 1951), p. 145-146.
[56] Monardes, *Joyfull Newes* (Frampton translation), pp. 38-44.
[57] Plate XX, Aegros curandi ratio (Method of treating the sick), by Jacques LeMoyne de Morgues in "Brevis Narratio eorum quae in Florida Americae provincia Gallis acciderunt," which is part 2 of Theodor de Bry's *Collectiones Peregrinationum in Indian Orientation* (Frankfurt, 1941). *Brevis Narratio* was translated into English by Fred B. Perkins as *The Narrative of LeMoyne* (Boston, 1875).
[58] Monardes, *Joyfull Newes* (Frampton translation), p. 83.
[59] AGI 54-5-17/68, fol. 14, SC.
[60] Gov. Francisco de Córcoles y Martínez of Florida to the Crown, St. Augustine, Nov. 16, 1706, fol. 5, AGI 58-1-28/12, SC.
[61] Gov. Antonio de Benavides of Florida to the Crown, St. Augustine, Sept. 28, 1727, fols. 6-7, AGI 58-1-31/14, SC.
[62] AGI 58-1-31/14, fols. 15-16, SC.
[63] Lt. Gov. Francisco Manuel de Roa of Havana to Secretary Antonio Ortiz de Otalora of the Council of the Indies, Havana, March 22, 1690, fols. 266-268, AGI 54-2-19/2, SC.
[64] Luis Rafael Arana, "The Day Governor Cabrera Left Florida," *Florida Historical Quarterly* 40 (October 1961), pp. 154-163.

FLORIDA DURING THE AMERICAN REVOLUTIONARY WAR
by Charles W. Arnade

One has to understand that the state of Florida of today—the twenty-seventh state to join the American Union—did not become a part of the United States until 1821, and then only as a territory. Statehood came in 1845. But this land called Florida was discovered, and from then became part of the continuous history of America, in 1513. From this date to 1821, Florida belonged to the Spanish colonial empire except for a twenty-year interlude from 1763 to 1783 when it became two additional English colonies, East and West Florida. Therefore, Florida was in English hands during the American Revolution. The history of Florida during the American War of Independence is unique and quite unknown to most Americans.

Florida became English at the conference table in Paris in 1763. The French were eliminated from the huge Mississippi waterways and valley in this peace treaty, and the Spanish-English dispute over the boundary between Georgia and Spanish Florida disappeared when Florida became English. Thus, the new English authorities could readjust and mark definite Florida borders. First they divided Florida into East and West Florida along the Apalachicola river, with St. Augustine the colonial seat of East Florida and Pensacola of West Florida. They extended West Florida to the eastern shores of the Mississippi, excluding New Orleans. The northern border of West and East Florida was the thirty-first parallel and the St. Mary's River at the extreme eastern end. In the 1763 peace treaty, all land west of the Mississippi, at least up to the Ohio, was considered Spanish, which meant that most of French Louisiana, excepting the portion east of the Mississippi, became Spanish. This meant that Mobile and the small settlements of Baton Rouge and Biloxi and the fort of Manchac just a few miles north of Baton Rouge became a part of West Florida.

Very soon West Florida was enlarged by including some disputed western Indian land. The northern border was moved to a straight line starting at the junction of the Yazoo and Mississippi rivers and running east to the Chattahoochee River. This line is variously identified as 32′ 30‛, 32′ 28‛, and by Whitaker as 32′ 26‛. Then the border ran south along the Chattahoochee and Apalachicola rivers to 31′ 30‛, where East Florida started. This addition to West Florida was now called the Yazoo Strip and included a series of small forts or blockhouses on the eastern shores of the Mississippi, facing the Spanish side in Spanish Louisiana.

These forts included Fort Panmure, called also Fort Rosalie, which later became Natchez; and at the most northern point near the junction of the Yazoo and Mississippi stood Fort Nogales renamed Walnut Hill, which is now Vicksburg. The Spanish historian, Zapatero, also speaks of a "Fort Thompson," probably on the "Thompson's Creek," cited by Holmes.

By 1764 the two Floridas had become true English colonies. The Spanish populations, mostly in Pensacola and St. Augustine, had almost all left. They were fearful for their Catholicism more than their loyalty to Spain. New people, mostly English or English-speaking Americans from the other colonies including the English Caribbean, came to the Floridas. But it must be made clear that Florida under the Spanish and the English never had a large population, either native or European. As a matter of fact, the least populated county of Florida today has more inhabitants than the whole European population of old Spanish Florida or the combined English East and West Florida. The larger, native, Indian population was also very sparse. Therefore, we are talking about a vast area—present-day Florida and large parts of Alabama, Mississippi, and a small section of Louisiana, but with few people according to today's standards. At the outbreak of the American Revolution, the Floridas were the least inhabited area of the English colonies in North America.

When discussing the two Floridas during the American Revolution we must be reminded that only thirteen of the English colonies in North America united in rebellion against the motherland. Others did not, such as huge Quebec (much larger than today), Nova Scotia (larger too), Newfoundland, rich Bermuda, the Bahamas, and the two Floridas. All

Florida During the American Revolutionary War

attempts by the revolutionary leaders to convince these colonies to join the rebellion fell on deaf ears. Bermuda, the Bahamas, and Newfoundland, with their insularity, were far more conservative, stable, and removed from the grievances of the continental English colonies. Their slow, or even lack of, evolution toward independence from England in the twentieth century is good proof of this.

Any good Canadian history textbook will give the obvious reasons why Quebec and Nova Scotia did not join the Revolution. The fears of the Catholic French Canadians had been calmed by the new English masters in the Quebec Act of 1774. But this Act had caused new antagonisms in the old Anglo-Saxon English colonies, including a wave of anti-Catholicism. It was only natural, then, that Quebec was not interested in joining the Revolution, but also quite fearful of the revolutionaries in these Anglo-Saxon colonies. This religious issue overshadowed all other causes in Quebec.

Nova Scotia was another case. It might be useful to consider Nova Scotia. Often the position of the Floridas and that of Nova Scotia at the beginning and during the American War of Independence are carefully compared. This is valid. It should be recalled that Nova Scotia then meant more or less the area now occupied by the three Canadian Atlantic provinces: Nova Scotia, New Brunswick, and Prince Edward Island. One must recall that old Nova Scotia had been an early colonial battlefield between France and England, just as Florida had been between Spain and England. By the time of the Revolution there had developed some similarity in the populations of the Floridas, especially of East Florida, and Nova Scotia. Each was the natural extension, to the south and north, of the thirteen rebellious colonies. Their union to the Revolution would have brought independence from the mouth of the St. Lawrence to the Florida Keys. But the Floridas and Nova Scotia, on the geographical extremes, were sparsely populated. It is true that Nova Scotia, whose population was scattered through isolated communities, did have around 17,000 people compared to 5,500 Europeans and 2,000 Negroes for both Floridas, mostly concentrated in Pensacola and St. Augustine. Still, all of these colonies were underpopulated compared to the thirteen rebellious colonies where, for example, South Carolina—less important than Virginia, Massachusetts, or New York—had over 100,000 inhabitants.

The three colonies, the two Floridas and Nova Scotia, felt little concern over the grievances that agitated the other colonies. Whatever grievances they had did not constitute "common ground" with those of the thirteen colonies. The one overriding cause against England of the thirteen colonies was the closing of the West for European settlement. This was of no importance to Nova Scotia, according to Canadian historians. It also was unimportant to East Florida. In the two Floridas, the new English authorities had established a good relationship with the Indians. It was so good that the English authorities of West Florida, including the Yazoo Strip with western Indians (the old West), had authority over the Indian land up to the Ohio River. Indian problems were minimal in Nova Scotia.

English taxation was little resented in the three colonies, mainly because it was not such a burden and, furthermore, its enforcement was quite lax. As a matter of fact, the royal officials of the three colonies were quite tolerant with the affairs of the whole population, European, Indian, and black. Pensacola, St. Augustine, and Halifax all had military garrisons and naval centers due to their strategic locations on the fringes of the English empire. The loyalty of these forces was very strong. They appeared to have had the support of the colonial settlers. John Adams is said to have stated angrily that the inhabitants of these colonies were "a set of fugitives and vagabonds who are also kept in fear by a fleet and an army." Adams was upset at the refusal of these colonies to join the Revolution. Because of such a sparse population, East Florida, West Florida, and Nova Scotia received direct financial grants voted by Parliament. Usually the subsidies for these three colonies were nearly identical. In 1763 it was £5,700 each for East and West Florida and £5,703 for Nova Scotia. All this might explain why no forceful leaders carrying the banner for the Revolution emerged in the three colonies. Later, the large addition of loyalist refugees to Nova Scotia and East Florida strengthened the royalist sentiments.

There were some basic differences. The two Floridas, just like Quebec, had only become English in 1763. Therefore, when the Revolution started, these colonies had been in English hands a single decade. Their settlers were all new, and the grievances that led to the Revolution in the other colonies had no deep roots. These people had just arrived and were preoccupied with such problems as getting settled in their new semitropical environment. More than in any other English colony in North America and the Caribbean the Floridas did not have a body of merchants, and trading hardly existed. All of them were either officeholders or recent arrivals who hoped to make a living from the soil, plus a number of adventurers attracted by the empty subtropics.

The Floridas for the first part of the English rule did not even have a

Florida During the American Revolutionary War

colonial assembly or legislature. In Nova Scotia it had come into existence in 1758. Florida had no tradition of representative rule. During the long Spanish rule neither St. Augustine nor Pensacola nor any other settlement had even a *cabildo*. When the War of Independence started, the Floridas did not have one iota of experience in their whole history with even limited, local self-government. The lack of an assembly in the Floridas as compared to Nova Scotia did produce one interesting difference. While the sentiments in the Floridas were quite anti-revolutionary and were even translated into some military action, in Nova Scotia there was an overwhelming desire to keep neutral. The settlers there decided to make neutrality a positive political and economic policy, hopefully bringing economic benefits, peace, and survival. This did not occur in the Floridas, where the English authorities ruled and the people obeyed.

The American War of Independence which turned into a world war of the great powers, including Spain, affected East and West Florida differently. Of interest is that, while East Florida had only about one-third of the population of West Florida, the literature in the annals of Florida history is more precise for East Florida. This is probably because West Florida eventually became parts of four different states. With a more heterogeneous population, it is rather a stepchild of American history, and no state claims full parenthood.

English rule of West Florida lasted only for eighteen years, until 1781. The famous American-born naturalist, William Bartram, in his journey through West Florida in 1778 found no revolutionary sympathy. While East Florida was exposed to revolutionary Georgia and a hostile revolutionary navy, West Florida also faced Spain in New Orleans and across the Mississippi, plus dissatisfied French settlers of old French Louisiana who resented the new Spanish rule. When Spain joined France in the war against England, then the fate of West Florida was sealed.

The first English governor of West Florida was Capt. George Johnstone who came to Pensacola in February 1764 with a British regiment. He was Scottish, and with him came Highlanders from South Carolina and New York. He was strong-minded, daring, "pugnacious," but also an excellent administrator. Forcefully he welded the diverse new colony into a strong unit. To woo the French, he guaranteed their old land titles if they would stay and improve their land. He also established unusually friendly relationships with the Indians, guided by the capable superintendent of Indian Affairs for the Southern Department, Col. John Stuart. Kynerd writes that West Florida was selected "as a testing ground for the new British-Indian policy which resulted from the Proclamation of 1763." This was the policy which originated such intense dislike by the white settlers in the thirteen rebellious colonies. Johnstone and Stuart journeyed all over the colony to meet with the Indians. Indian congresses met at Mobile and Pensacola in 1765, representing the various ethnic groups such as the important Creeks, Chickasaws, and Choctaws, and minor groupings. The two Englishmen were determined that the Indians should be treated fairly by merchants and traders. In other matters, the English governor was dedicated to enlarge and beautify Pensacola and offered free lots to petitioners who, quoting Caruso, agreed "to fence and build on it a sizeable home with a brick chimney." Howard reminds us that, before the English arrived, Pensacola "was a small village consisting of about one hundred huts encircled by a stockade." Johnstone was particularly interested in strengthening and enlarging the Mississippi forts and blockhouses.

By November 1766 it was agreed, after some opposition, to install the first session of the West Florida Assembly, which met in Pensacola, and the representative from Mobile was elected speaker. This was the first legislative body in the Floridas and antedates by many years the one in East Florida. In part, the assembly was called by the Governor to help his sagging popularity. It did not do so. Johnstone's "pugnacious" character led to interminable quarrels with his political and, especially, military subordinates. He was forced out of office early in 1767. Three years of executive confusion followed. His successor committed suicide. In August 1770, Peter Chester, a veteran of many years in the army, arrived; and with him administrative order again reigned. Chester was the West Florida governor during the American Revolution and Spanish invasion of the colony.

Professor Johnson says that the beginning of the War of Independence "was scarcely felt in West Florida." There were no revolutionaries or American sympathizers. Yet West Florida was wrested from the English. One should recall the interesting and complex foreign policy of the great powers as a consequence of the American War of Independence. Every American schoolboy knows that France became an ally of the American revolutionaries. What is often forgotten is that in 1779 Spain entered the war against England and technically became an ally of the revolutionaries. The French and Spanish participations were crucial to West Florida.

Florida During the American Revolutionary War

In 1761, France and Spain had signed the Family Compact. This "family alliance" had been costly to Spain owing to the defeat of France, joined by Spain in 1761, in the French-Indian Wars (called in European history the "Seven Year's War"). Here Spain lost Florida to England. Still, Professor Bemis believes that the Family Compact was "the polestar of each monarch's foreign policy." But when war was made against the English by the American revolutionaries, Spain showed only an apprehensive enthusiasm. On the one side there was, in the words of Bemis, "exultant rejoicing," since England was Spain's archenemy. If England should win, it would be at tremendous cost. If the Americans won, the Spanish were erroneously convinced, the new nation would be weak and Spain would have a chance of regaining lost lands in North America and solidifying their claims to the Mississippi and Ohio valleys. On the other hand, Spain "had the largest and most vulnerable empire in the New World." If Spain sided with the Americans their colonial subjects also might demand the right of independence.

As Bemis remarked, supported by Yela, to Spain this whole matter of the American Revolution had to be considered "merely a tool in Spain's European international combinations, a tool with sharp and dangerous edges, to be handled with care and caution." For example, at first in 1776, Charles III gave financial subsidies through the French "to pour oil in the flames of insurrection." But extraordinary measures were taken, according to Yela, "to conceal the operation and to avoid the appearance of assistance to colonies rebelling against European dominion."

Then there were, also, the underlying tensions between Spain and France, although united by the Family Compact. Spain had not forgotten that France had dragged Spain into a disastrous war over a decade earlier. Spain wanted to get even with England, but mainly in Europe. That was far more important than any area in America. First of all she wanted to get back Gibraltar, then Minorca, and also to attack Portugal, the traditional ally of England. France was not anxious to be compromised in a war in Europe and, especially, in the Iberian Peninsula. In 1777, "the proud Murcian, Floridablanca," assumed foreign affairs for Spain, and he showed extreme caution and skepticism for any kind of involvement in the Revolutionary War at the side of France. He wanted good relations with Portugal and was opposed to the independence of the thirteen rebellious American colonies; but he was willing to continue secret subsidies to prolong the war, hoping for a weakened England in order to gain concessions through diplomatic pressure. Then the American victory of Saratoga in October 1777, changed all of this. For France, it was now or never to get even with England in America. Floridablanca was still dubious and was still resisting French pressure to join her in going to war against England. In the face of Spanish reluctance, France slowly increased the bounty for Spain's entrance in the war, assuring Spain the reconquest of Jamaica and Florida, including all of West Florida (which included the old Louisiana enclave east of the Mississippi and the Yazoo Strip). France even talked about Spain gaining fishing rights in Newfoundland and, finally, the reconquest of Minorca.

Floridablanca was unimpressed. Only Gibraltar mattered. He was interested in Minorca, but Spain would only enter the war for one price, Gibraltar; Minorca would be welcome; the American reconquests and fishery in Newfoundland were uninteresting. For Minorca alone as a price in Europe, the gamble of a doubtful victory was too much. Floridablanca was so intent on Gibraltar that he even approached England with an offer of strict neutrality (probably meaning no more subsidies to the Americans) if Gibraltar was returned to Spain. When war broke out between England and France in 1778, Spain immediately offered to mediate for the price of Gibraltar, but England refused to talk about Gibraltar.

England's refusal, and France's heightened proposal to help Spain in getting Gibraltar, led to the entry of Spain into the war after signing the Convention of Aranjuez in June 1779. France would not make peace until Gibraltar and Minorca had been restored to Spain. France also volunteered aid to Spain in securing the expulsion of the British from parts of the Gulf coast of Central America. And, if France regained Newfoundland, Spain would have fishing rights. Interestingly, Florida was not mentioned except for "the possession of the river and fort of Mobile, Florida." On June 21, 1779, Spain declared war on England, but did not recognize the independence of the United States. She simply joined the war as an ally of the French.

"The river and fort of Mobile" were, as we know, close to New Orleans, and in 1779 Louisiana with New Orleans were in the hands of the Spanish as a result of the Peace Treaty of 1763, a treaty in which the English had been given free navigation of the Mississippi. At the beginning, Spain had difficulty asserting its sovereignty in New Orleans and Louisiana. The old French settlers did not want the Spanish, and much trouble developed.

Florida During the American Revolutionary War

On New Years Day of 1777, however, the year of the Battle of Saratoga, the forceful and brilliant Bernardo de Gálvez (after whom Galveston is named) became governor of Louisiana. He would play a key role in the American War of Independence. In 1777 he was only twenty-nine years old but already had a distinguished career. One of the few Spaniards who was sympathetic to the American Revolution, he opened contact with the revolutionaries long before 1779. He made navigation on the Mississippi difficult for the English, but easy for the revolutionaries. Long before the Spanish declaration of war of June 1779, he assisted the revolutionaries in the old West with arms and provisions and made New Orleans, in the words of Caruso, "a base of operation against the English." Many American revolutionaries traveled to and conspired from New Orleans. Young and daring Gálvez could take these liberties, disliked by the cold, stiff, and elder Floridablanca, because he was the favorite nephew of José de Gálvez who occupied the high position of minister (sometimes called executive secretary) of the Indies, the office in charge of all American colonial affairs.

Basically, Gálvez acted for the self-interest of Spain and Louisiana rather than ideological sympathy with the American Revolution. He was first astounded and then worried about the weakness of Spanish Louisiana and he considered a new war with England inevitable. Consequently, in the last part of 1777 and all through 1778, New Orleans became a base of operation for the revolutionaries who sailed up and down the Mississippi attacking, burning, and looting the English forts, blockhouses, settlements, and plantations along the English shores, especially of West Florida. The best known of these was the James Willing contingent of about one hundred men who operated in the February and spring of 1778. Other American rebels connected with Willing's men captured two English vessels from their New Orleans sanctuary. The English governor of West Florida, Chester, strongly complained and "demanded that Gálvez explain his unneutral conduct." Gálvez was quite evasive, but then agreed on a token return of certain goods seized.

Governor Chester became aware of the exposed position of West Florida. He realized that Gálvez was anxious to occupy the colony, especially the English shore of the Mississippi and, hopefully, Mobile and Pensacola. Chester requested urgent reinforcements from everywhere but, mainly, from Jamaica. Matters moved slowly. After delays, the supreme English commander in North America, Gen. Henry Clinton, agreed to dispatch three thousand troops to West and East Florida. In mid-January of 1779, twelve hundred men, which included about five hundred loyalists from the revolutionary colonies and the rest German mercenaries, arrived in West Florida. A great number of them were to defend the Mississippi line. Was it too late?

In June, Spain entered the War. The English command ordered an attack on Louisiana. But Gálvez had received the news of the declaration of war considerably earlier than the civil and military authorities in West Florida. Gálvez, who was ready, did not delay, and began the attack. Rapidly he took the English forts on the Mississippi, then defeated an English column marching on Louisiana. He stopped his advance to prepare the capture of Mobile. In the initial stage he had won the Mississippi eastern shore and ruined the English Louisiana invasion campaign, which never got off the ground. In 1780 he took Mobile, and thus all important points in West Florida except Pensacola were now in Gálvez' hand.

The Spanish leader, knowing that the fight for Pensacola would not be easy, decided on careful preparations. Mobile became the base for his preparation. The English were unable to retake Mobile in January 1781. Gálvez became impatient with the slowness in the arrival of reinforcements, and so he himself rushed to Havana to expedite the campaign. By the end of February Gálvez was finally ready to start his attack. It was a two-directional operation in which a "small armada" came from Havana and a larger contingent converged from Mobile and New Orleans. On March 9, the battle of Pensacola had started, which, Rush claims, "was a decisive factor in the outcome of the Revolution." The battle lasted exactly two months. By mid-April an unexpected third force arrived, "a combined French and Spanish squadron." Gálvez as supreme commander now had over seven thousand men opposed by only twenty-five hundred English. The outcome was never in doubt although the English put up a good fight. Rush writes that "it was one of the most brilliantly executed battles of the War. With the fall of Pensacola to the Spanish, Great Britain lost a very important military base and harbor, her last remaining foothold in the Gulf of Mexico."

While the siege of Pensacola was in its last stages, English settlers around Natchez, Baton Rouge, and Manchac tried to recapture key military posts; after some initial success the attempt failed. On May 8, 1781, the English authorities in West Florida surrendered, thereby returning all of West Florida to Spain. Its ultimate fate was to be determined at the next peace treaty.

Florida During the American Revolutionary War [105]

The surrender terms offered by Gálvez, writes Abbey Hanna, "were exceedingly generous, not to say lenient." The American revolutionaries and the French felt Gálvez' leniency was "extraordinary, objectionable and alarming." The English garrison were not made prisoners, based on a pledge that they would not fight against the Spanish anymore.

The diary of Francisco de Miranda, who participated in the siege and victory of Pensacola from April 19, does not mention, nor have an opinion about, the surrender terms of Gálvez. The appearance of Miranda in the West Florida campaign is of special significance. Francisco de Miranda is one of the best-known figures of Latin American independence. He has gone down in history as "World Citizen" and "the Precursor of South American Independence." He was the "intellectual leader" of the Spanish American War of Independence; he is the Thomas Paine of Spanish America. This Venezuelan was born in Caracas on March 28, 1750. Therefore, when he arrived in Pensacola with the combined French and Spanish fleet in April 1781, he was thirty years old. An agitated past lay behind him and a more forceful future was in store. Only Simón Bolívar, his acquaintance, fellow *caraqueño,* and in the end his rival, ranks higher or at least equal in the annals of the history of Hispanic America.

Miranda joined the Spanish armed forces in 1772 and was sent to a frontier post in Africa where he took part in the Algerian campign of 1774-1775. He felt that his services there were not rewarded, while inept superiors were given decorations. One author writes, "It is undeniable that from this hour forward Francisco was a restless and disgruntled soldier." While on leave, he visited Gibraltar and became enchanted with "Anglo-Saxon culture." In 1780 he was transferred to America where he eventually became an aide-de-camp of Gen. Juan Manuel de Cagigal who was acting governor of Cuba and a man that Miranda admired.

Cagigal was in charge of the land forces carried by the combined French and Spanish fleet that arrived in mid-April 1781 in Pensacola to decisively aid the attack and siege of Pensacola led by Gálvez. Miranda still was Cagigal's adjutant. As said, Miranda kept a diary, one detailed from the day of departure to the capture of Pensacola; it is mainly military in nature and remains a key document of the Battle of Pensacola. Miranda was promoted to a temporary lieutenant colonel because of services rendered in the Pensacola campaign. He returned with Cagigal to Havana. There he became attached to the French admiral, Joseph Paul de Grasse, who played the key role in the English defeat of Yorktown. It is said that Miranda's charm, daring, and shrewdness was responsible for additional needed cash to the French admiral for his Yorktown maneuver. As Thorning writes, "If Admiral de Grasse deserves to be honored as one of the 'Heroes of Yorktown,' the South American [Miranda] who helped him with food and money at Havana, can have some share in the glory." And Nuceté-Sardi states, "In this fashion, Colonel Miranda contributed his share to the definite triumph in the struggle for North American Independence." He also played a key role in the Pensacola campaign that led to reoccupation of West Florida.

With the success of the Battle of Pensacola and the English surrender of West Florida, the Spanish were reluctant to undertake further military actions in Florida or, for that matter, in the Revolutionary War. The Irish-Spanish Arturo O'Neill assumed the governorship of West Florida, responsible to the governor of Louisiana. Until the peace treaty, he made no efforts to occupy the area between Pensacola and the Apalachicola River nor the central and eastern stretches of the Yazoo Strip. It always had been primarily, and now was more than ever, Indian land.

The English were still in East Florida. The events here during the Revolutionary War were quite different from those of West Florida. Initially, East Florida was governed by another Scotsman, the placid, charming, and humane Gov. James Grant. He lacked the dynamism of his fellow Scotsman, Johnstone of West Florida. Grant was not "pugnacious" and got along well with practically everyone. He, as Johnstone, was on good terms with the Indians, now the Seminoles in this region. This colony, large in area but with a tiny population, was made by Grant a place of much merriment. He said in private correspondence that St. Augustine was now "the gayest Place in America, nothing but Balls, Assemblies and Concerts, we are too inconsiderable to enter Politicks and Faction...." No doubt this is somewhat exaggerated. A tiny community, and so isolated, creates petty squabbles. Such had been the case with Spanish St. Augustine and it was still true with English St. Augustine, but much reduced during Grant's term due to his splendid personality. To be sure, the establishment of a new colony south of St. Augustine of foreign elements and Catholic persuasion—Italians, Minorcans, and Greeks—created new dissentions. But this was unrelated to the issues of the other English colonies which culminated in the Revolutionary War.

If Governor Grant's words might be unrealistic there is no doubt that documentary evidence shows East Florida to have been a new English colony removed from the turmoil of the other thirteen colonies to the

Florida During the American Revolutionary War [107]

north and also more tranquil than English West Florida. There was a discussion, rather subdued, about the polite unwillingness of the Governor to establish an elected assembly as had been done in West Florida by Johnstone and which was within the power of Grant to do. His commission certainly gave him the discretion of "the summoning of an assembly," which he considered "impractical for the time" because of the small population. He considered his council of ten officials and distinguished citizens sufficient. Two of the closest friends and associates of Grant were partisans for an assembly, but this issue did not create a heated controversy.

In July 1771, Grant left for England due to bad health, and he finally resigned his governorship in April 1773. On March 1, 1774, his permanent successor, Patrick Tonyn, arrived in St. Augustine. Mowat reminds us that the arrival of Tonyn was a fortnight before "Lord North was to introduce in Parliament the bill to close the port of Boston." Tonyn's term coincided with the Revolutionary War. This great revolt was of much concern to East Florida as an Atlantic Coast colony. The personality of Tonyn was diametrically opposed to that of Grant. He was sullen, introvert, quarrelsome; disdainful of nearly everyone. Yet he was a good, tough administrator. The new governor also was totally loyal to the English Crown and had an intense dislike for the revolutionaries.

Tonyn was universally disliked except by some few who depended on his favors. If revolutionary sentiment would have existed, Tonyn's personality would have been to their advantage. But this was not the case. This shows that there was no grassroot support for American independence. Opposition did develop, but Mowat writes that this "was a party in opposition to the governor.... Whatever the causes and extent of faction in the province, it was certainly not such as to menace its loyalty in a serious way. All main currents carried it toward the loyal shore." Every source one consults states that when the news of the Declaration of Independence reached St. Augustine, John Hancock and Sam Adams were hung in effigy.

There is no doubt that when the Revolutionary War started its leaders were anxious for the support and capture of East Florida. Georgia and South Carolina were fearful of a royalist Florida. Military action was always contemplated by both sides, but it never amounted to much. The revolutionary authorities in Georgia always were worried about East Florida, more so when St. Augustine became a haven for loyalists, mainly from the southern revolutionary colonies. Katherine Hanna writes that "the Georgians sought to impress the revolutionary commander with the concept that their concern in the war was not the British troops in the North but the border situation with Florida."

No serious military action developed. Mowat, who has done the most detailed study of English Florida, calls the small military activities between East Florida and Georgia and South Carolina "a little dirty petite guerre." Congressman Charles Bennett, an able amateur historian, calls his recent monograph "The Southernmost Battlefields of the Revolution." First of all, the number of armed forces in East Florida was amazingly low, fluctuating from just one hundred to never more than two hundred fifty between 1775 and 1780. The revolutionaries in Georgia and South Carolina, although encouraged by a resolution of the Continental Congress of January 1776, never were able to muster a force to really invade East Florida as the Spaniards had done in West Florida.

Plans by Governor Tonyn to invade Georgia also came to nothing, even though he created his own "provincial corps" which he called the East Florida Rangers. It was basically made up of adventurers and hatefilled royalist refugees from Georgia and South Carolina. The corps amounted to about one hundred thirty men. This Tonyn force created confusion and controversy in East Florida and strengthened the anti-Tonyn faction. The military authorities considered Tonyn's Rangers paramilitary and unlawful, and the controversy went all the way to the English commander in America, Gen. William Howe. In 1779, Tonyn lost control over his Rangers; they were absorbed into the military units, but Tonyn henchmen were not given commissions.

All this squabbling made the actual warfare against Georgia only a minor skirmish. The years of 1776 and 1777 produced raids on both sides. The most tangible result was the capture of cattle. There were some raids on plantations and settlements all along the Florida-Georgia border. These types of violent activities had also taken place in the past, previous to the Revolutionary War. Now they only intensified.

Recently there has been some dispute as to the historical importance of these skirmishes and the somewhat bigger clashes of 1778. Pennington has given us a good selection of Tonyn's letters of this period dealing with the Governor's "defence" and "retaliating" expeditions, his loyalty to his Rangers, and his attempt to recruit as many Indians as possible. Bennett's monograph reminds the reader that this fight "remains poorly understood or virtually unknown" and is of "significance that should not be ignored in the larger drama of the American Revolution." England "fragmented

Florida During the American Revolutionary War

her strength and dispersed her forces," which was the basic reason for the forthcoming defeat at Yorktown. Mowat fails to ascribe his "petitte guerre" this importance. The 1776 raids were mostly cattle raids. By June 4, 1776, the King's birthday, the frontier was so quiet that the English had "a regatta on the St. Johns River." In 1777, the skirmishes were resumed and in February a small contingent of "regulars" plus Tonyn's Rangers and some Seminoles made a dash into Georgia and captured an American stockade, "Fort McIntosh," on the Satilla River. They captured sixty-eight rebels and about two thousand head of cattle. Five men died: four Americans and one Seminole. In May, the Americans talked about a forthcoming powerful invasion force, but it ended in a small skirmish where a tiny American force was totally defeated.

The year 1778 witnessed a slight increase in military activities on the Florida-Georgia border. There were again talks on both sides about invasions, further stimulated by another call from the Continental Congress advising the capture of East Florida. In March, a Florida raiding party captured and burned an American fort on the Altamaha, taking twenty-three prisoners. The next month, a small naval engagement occurred in the waters of St. Simon Island and two American ships fell into English hands.

By June 1778 the Americans had assembled a rather impressive force of over two thousand men from South Carolina and Georgia, led by the capable revolutionary, Gen. Robert Howe, and supported by some naval units. An advanced force crossed the St. Mary's River dividing Georgia and East Florida. After some intense fighting it appeared that the Americans had the upper hand, but their luck changed when the English forces stood firm. The Americans became discouraged, their command disunited and their ranks weakened; they decided to retreat into Georgia. There was no "way for a patriot conquest of Florida." General Howe considered the whole expedition "a fiasco," and he said it was "one of the most unfortunate incidents of my life." They, the Americans, did not try again. The actual casualties were only a few dozen for both sides.

The next action was the largest and most important operation yet, and culminated in the occupation of Savannah in the winter of 1778 by the English forces. It was a new phase beyond the "petite guerre," in which St. Augustine became the base of departure for a new campaign which took the war away from East Florida. The late 1778 operation was labeled by historian Commager as "amphibious." It was organized from New York and led by Brigadier Archibald Campbell. He was aided by British troops from East Florida under the command of the Swiss Brig. Gen., Augustine Prevost. It was Prevost who was much at odds with Tonyn. The combined English forces which included Tonyn's Rangers, after some initial difficulty, defeated the Georgians. With the capture of Savannah by Campbell, "a royal governor was reinstated who summoned an assembly and virtually restored the state to the British Empire." Prevost, to the delight of Tonyn, was transferred to Savannah. But this victory was the end of Tonyn's Rangers, which the English command abolished.

The victorious English troops led by Prevost marched into South Carolina, leaving a trail of blood and tears. French naval forces joined the battle, counterattacking in Georgia and South Carolina. In the end, by 1780, active warfare had come to Georgia and South Carolina and had removed East Florida from any fighting. By May 1780, East Florida celebrated what is by some considered the "worst disaster of the War to the American arms" when the English campaign, which had started partially in St. Augustine, resulted in the capture of Charleston and the taking of over five thousand prisoners.

There was no time to rejoice in East Florida about the reestablishment of royalist rule in Georgia and South Carolina. As stated, in June 1779 Spain had entered the war against England and Gálvez was invading West Florida. If the threat from Georgia and South Carolina was temporarily eliminated, sudden fears about Spanish actions, such as a large invasion of East Florida, took hold of the English in St. Augustine. The Spanish danger was taken more seriously than any previous worries about the American revolutionaries. Looking at it now from an historical vantage, it is fair to say that the American threat was underestimated and the Spanish danger was overemphasized.

No doubt the Spanish had serious designs to reconquer both Floridas. Efforts to maintain the loyalty of the Indians were undertaken all through the twenty years of English rule. They were accelerated with the beginnings of the Revolutionary War. Documents published by Boyd and Navarro give us glances of these Spanish contacts with the Indians. But the Florida Indians (Seminole and Creeks) failed to show much enthusiasm, with the exception of a few Lower Creeks near the Gulf coast who traded with and journeyed intermittently to Havana. As the Revolutionary War progressed, Spain's contact with the Floridas expanded to more ambitious intelligence activities. Historian Kathryn Abbey Hanna, in several studies accomplished by painstaking research, has

Florida During the American Revolutionary War

thoroughly documented these Spanish attempts and designs, but there are still many gaps. Spanish agents had been sent to the revolutionaries and to the loyalist colonies. In 1776, the governor of Cuba was ordered to gather intelligent, trusted agents in Florida and Jamaica. Funds, modest to be sure, were appropriated for such a purpose. Governor Gálvez of Louisiana used many agents previous to his West Florida invasion.

The first agent to arrive in St. Augustine was a certain Miguel Josef Chapuz, a fisherman who was dispatched to St. Augustine to "bring sacred oil" which the Catholic Church in Havana was authorized to send to the few Catholics in St. Augustine. He carried secret instructions to a Spanish resident of St. Augustine, Luciano de Herrera. He gathered useful data, and so the Spanish governor in Havana was aware of most of the military activities on the Florida-Georgia border.

In 1777, two commissioners were dispatched directly to North America, one as an observer to the Continental Congress and the other, disguised as a naturalist, to St. Augustine. This was Josef Elixio de la Puente, who had lived in Florida previous to 1763. This gentleman should not be confused, as has been done, with his equally or more distinguished brother, Juan Elixio de la Puente, who had served as the real estate agent and unofficial voice of the departing Spaniards in 1763 and whose St. Augustine map and real estate descriptions have been the basis of today's Historical Reconstruction of St. Augustine. Juan was now an important government auditor in the Tribunal de Cuentas in Havana and recommended his brother Josef for the intelligence assignment in St. Augustine. Juan, according to Boyd and Navarro, was "a prominent advocate of the lost province of East Florida." Also, Juan was the key individual in Havana's contact with the Florida Indians during the English occupation. Josef's early reports are missing. He left Havana in December 1777 and arrived in St. Augustine, but nothing was heard from him until May 1778. Further summer reports arrived in Havana after that. He showed definite partisanship for the revolutionaries, and this colored his evaluation. He predicted the victory of the revolutionary forces of General Howe in 1778 and stated that he was remaining in St. Augustine to greet the revolutionary invasion force. The Spanish governor reprimanded him for erroneous judgments. He was reminded to stay with the British even if St. Augustine fell into American hands.

After September 1778 the actions and whereabouts of Josef Elixio de la Puente are obscure and confusing. All we know is that he died early in 1780 in revolutionary territory. Probably he must be considered the

Spanish Floridian most useful to the American Revolution. He and his brother Juan should be counted with Miranda and Gálvez as men who aided the Revolution; the two brothers were closest to the Florida scene. The Florida historian Mark Boyd, aided by the Spanish historian José Navarro la Torre, worked on a lengthy scholarly study of Juan and Josef Elixio de la Puente which remains unfinished due to Boyd's death.

The English victory of Charleston in May 1780 was short-lived. It started the fateful march of Gen. Charles Cornwallis from Charleston through Virginia and ended in the crucial defeat of the English at the hands of the Americans and French at Yorktown in October 1781, to which Miranda had contributed indirectly. After the defeat at Yorktown, English hopes for a victory or peace based on the status quo or *uti possidentis* disappeared. Peace negotiations and diplomatic maneuvers in Europe now overshadowed any military activities.

Even before the news of Yorktown had reached St. Augustine, the news of the fall of Pensacola had arrived by mid-summer of 1781. Then in the late fall the news of Yorktown arrived, and by the spring of 1782 further bad news arrived. The English had decided to evacuate Charleston and all of Florida. The situation in East Florida was, at the best, tense and, at the worst, near panic. The last chapter of English Florida had started. Excitement and tensions now came to the placid colony as never before in its whole history.

The tranquility of St. Augustine and with it East Florida, was really interrupted for the first time as a consequence of the English victory of Charleston in 1780. It should be stated that St. Augustine as early as September 1776 received some American prisoners from the Virginia campaign. They were put inside the powerful fort built over a century earlier by the Spaniards, but were later transferred to the sloop *Otter* which was converted into a prison ship. The number and doings of these prisoners are not too clear. To the few Americans were added French and Spanish seamen wrecked in Florida waters or even mere adventurers or small-time buccaneers. We are told that when English rule ended in East Florida they accounted for nearly three hundred individuals simply classified as prisoners. Many of them might not have had anything to do with the Revolutionary War.

Excitement came when over sixty American revolutionaries from the Charleston recapture were later transferred by Cornwallis to St. Augustine because they had violated their status as parolees. Manucy tells us, "The roster of prisoners from Charleston reads like a contemporary

Florida During the American Revolutionary War

Who's Who." Over twenty of these Carolinians were members of the South Carolina Assembly; others were lawyers, surgeons, schoolmasters, and high-ranking members of the South Carolina militia. Three of the prisoners had signed the American Declaration of Independence: Arthur Middleton, Edward Rutledge, and Thomas Heyward, Jr. This last gentleman left an imprint in Florida history, as he precipitated the only patriotic episode of the English Floridas during the War of Independence.

Heyward was a young planter versed in law who had actively fought in battle against the English. Many of his fellow Carolinians continued their status as parolees and moved freely, living either in the unfinished government house or as private boarders. A few who were considered untrustworthy were imprisoned in the fort. Not so Heyward. He and a few others received permission to celebrate the Fourth of July of 1781, They organized a small and intimate banquet which ended with a tasty English plum pudding topped with "a tiny flag with thirteen stars and stripes." Then Heyward asked the banqueters to sing a new national song he had composed which started, "God save the thirteen States, thirteen United States." It was to the melody of "God Save the King." This Heyward hymn, first sung at this Fourth of July dinner in 1871 in St. Augustine, was heard "afterward from Georgia to New Hampshire."

While most of these South Carolina gentlemen had considerable freedom, there were moments of danger and suspense for them. At one point they were classified as hostages, with the threat of death by hanging in retribution for threatened execution of English prisoners classified by the Americans as spies. There was much apprehension in St. Augustine, as the South Carolina prisoners and parolees had established much social intercourse in the town, which was always excited by newcomers due to its isolation and boredom. Nothing happened; neither side took action on its threats. By August 1781 the South Carolinians were exchanged and left St. Augustine for the revolutionary North. The one true presence of the American Revolution in the Floridas had ended.

The stay of the South Carolina elite prisoners for one year plus the fast-moving news from the war led to three new activities which certainly affected nearly everyone in East Florida. This was the establishment of the long-desired assembly, the arrival of the main bulk of the loyalist refugees, and the use of St. Augustine again for another military attack, but this time in the Caribbean. The request for an assembly had existed since the first year of English rule. Grant had politely opposed it. Tonyn's opposition was equal but more belligerent. The large anti-Tonyn faction used the assembly as their main fighting banner. The Governor told his superiors that "turbulent tempers and leveling principles common in American assemblies" would also be the nature of an East Florida assembly. But by mid-July 1779 Tonyn had changed his mind and recommended the summoning of the assembly. He now said that "the malignant spirit hath almost subsided."

The reasons for Tonyn's change were genuine. His personal enemies had failed to get him dismissed; danger of an invasion from Georgia by land and from South Carolina by sea had lessened. The Spanish intrigues and intelligence activities and Spain's entrance into the war were a real threat and possibility. There was need for unity among the English population instead of local squabbles and jealousies unrelated to the war. Tonyn thought that maybe an assembly would serve as an escape valve for accumulated pressures. Furthermore, loyalist refugees had arrived and more might be on the way, as was the case. Most of them had brought their black servants or slaves. Since there was in East Florida no code or rules for blacks, free or slave, Tonyn felt that an assembly should regulate this ever increasing population. That is one duty he did not cherish to perform by himself even with his autocratic disposition. He was instructed by the English authorities to call the assembly, after being told he already had such power and should not have asked. But then, again Tonyn changed his mind. The South Carolina parolees had arrived and he did not want an assembly in their presence. With their departure the road was finally clear.

In March, 1781 the first Assembly gathered. The upper chamber was the old Governor's Council and the lower house was composed of nineteen men elected by white males—all Protestants, twenty-one years or older, with ownership of at least fifty acres. Those elected needed these same qualifications but had to own a minimum of five hundred acres. Interestingly, the Assembly was dominated by the newcomers who had moved to East Florida because of the American Revolution. It was an assembly ruled by the loyalists from the colonies. This and the second assembly dealt mostly with internal problems and especially the blacks' problems—slavery and the drafting of blacks for the defense of East Florida.

The assemblies proved to be quite important in convincing the English authorities to hold East Florida after Yorktown, at which time it was decided to evacuate South Carolina and Georgia. There was no doubt when evacuation plans for South Carolina and Georgia were discussed by the English authorities and command that the possibility of including East

Florida During the American Revolutionary War [115]

Florida—the whole southern Atlantic coast—was part of the discussion. The assemblies were determined to stop this. It did not take much convincing because there were other matters, political and international, that overshadowed the military considerations.

Once East Florida was kept and the two other colonies given up, the problems of the sudden influx of loyalist refugees became acute. The influx became a flood after Yorktown and the evacuation of Savannah and Charleston. The arrival of the loyalists in East Florida is probably the best-known chapter in the history of Florida during the Revolutionary War; Professor Wilbur H. Siebert has produced detailed and lengthy studies on the subject. The early loyalists came when Georgia and South Carolina joined the Revolution. It is said that seven hundred arrived in 1778. Then when the English recaptured Savannah and Charleston the migration of St. Augustine stopped. But it resumed at a great pace after Yorktown. By March 1782 the British command evacuated the South, but East Florida was exempted mainly because England felt that East Florida was not a part of the American Revolution, and not territory for the United States but a possible negotiation issue with Spain. Furthermore, they needed St. Augustine as a place for the refugees.

By early 1783, the loyalist population in East Florida was nearly three times as large as the pre-Yorktown population. By the end of the English period in 1783, the new population was many times over the original English population of 1763-64: it stood at more than seventeen thousand inhabitants (excluding the Indians) of which about sixty percent were now blacks. Naturally, this created new and often serious problems, especially in St. Augustine. The colony had few if no natural resources available for consumption; housing was scarce; police forces and health facilities were inadequate; funds were lacking; speculation and inflation became acute. At the same time there was a "mushrooming growth" and there was a boom. For example, for the first time, a printed newspaper, the *East Florida Gazette*, made its appearance. Theatrical performances took place. St. Augustine had never seen such activities.

All this could not dispel the uncertainty of the colony and the probability that the days of English rule of East Florida were numbered. Only the pressure of all classes and factions in St. Augustine, including the Indians, plus the resolve not to turn the colony over to American rule had convinced the English authorities in North America and England to postpone the evacuation of East Florida. Furthermore, as said, St. Augustine should be preserved as an intermediate place for the refugees until the peace treaty. If Florida was lost it should go back to Spain at the negotiation table in Europe where it could be used as a bargaining territory.

One must also remember that news traveled slowly, especially to St. Augustine. The increased uncertainty created confusion, apprehension, rumors, and even disjointed military actions. This was the case of the small expedition led by the South Carolinian loyalist, Col. Andrew Deveaux. It was equipped and sailed from St. Augustine in the early spring of 1873, and on April 18 captured the Bahamas, returning it to English rule. Nassau and the Bahama chain had been captured in 1782 by a combined Spanish-French-American expedition in which Gálvez and Miranda had had a hand. Spain claimed it and a Spanish governor ruled from Nassau. Now it had been recaptured for the English by a loyalist from St. Augustine. The irony was that the Spanish surrender at Nassau took place a few days after the actual signing of the peace treaty in Paris which had given the Bahamas back to England. Consequently, the Deveaux expedition was the last military action of the war.

Some called the reconquest of the Bahamas the first act of peace. In Paris, the preliminaries of peace had been signed in January 1783. The United States accepted the treaty on April 15, 1783. The final treaty was signed on September 3, 1783. Yorktown had taken place in October 1781. This meant there were two years of negotiations. The English defeat at Yorktown led to the resignation of Prime Minister North who was succeeded by the Marquis of Rockingham in March 1782, with Lord Shelburne in charge of colonial affairs. In April of that year, Shelburne opened negotiations with Benjamin Franklin. In July 1872, after the death of Rockingham, Shelburne became prime minister. Anyhow, by April 1782 the real peace negotiations had started. It should be recalled that further military reverses by the English at the hands of the French in the Caribbean and in South Asia, and the recapture by Spain of Minorca, had made the necessity of peace for the English more necessary. Shelburne, who had "consistently opposed independence" for the Americans, was, in the words of Bemis, convinced by military events that the necessary price of peace was American independence, but perhaps some part of the colonies might yet be recovered by diplomacy. The Floridas' fate was strictly up to the negotiators in Europe.

The preliminary articles of peace were agreed upon at the end of November 1782, signed in January 1783, and the final peace treaty signed on September 3 of the same year. As we said, there was a span of nearly

Florida During the American Revolutionary War [117]

two years between Yorktown and September 3, 1783, and about one-and-a-half years between the time Shelburne met with Franklin and when Shelburne was willing to accept independence. Why was there the long delay? The interests and demands of France and Spain had to be considered and were often more important than the American problem. And then there was the matter of the borders of the new country and, here, France and Spain had definite opinions quite opposed to American hopes and expectations.

From the beginning of the peace talks some matters appeared certain. West Florida was already in Spanish hands and they were not ready to give it up. England was determined not to give East Florida to the Americans but to the Spaniards if necessary. Spain felt sure of the acquisition of East Florida in the peace negotiations, but the Floridas were never among the important issues. The Americans did not press their desire for the Floridas, especially East Florida, and they knew it was difficult to make the Spanish evacuate West Florida. The Americans were really more interested in Canada and fearful that it would revert back to France. Canada and the central and upper Mississippi and Ohio valleys and waterways were more important than the Floridas. The one area of Florida of some importance to them was the Yazoo Strip.

Spain was optimistic about both Floridas. Little or nothing was discussed about the Floridas except the matter of the Mississippi River, which dealt with western West Florida, and especially the Yazoo Strip. But here again, Spain was more concerned about the central Mississippi, Ohio, and Tennessee valleys, all above the Yazoo Strip. There was also the issue of the Gulf coast of Central America where England had acquired economic rights to cut wood (now about where Belize or British Honduras is). But the overriding issue for Spain was the return of Gibraltar, lost in a previous war. This is why Spain went to war in the first place. The American negotiators had shown no interest in the Gibraltar matter, and France was starting to show coolness to it as an issue. She was reluctant to continue the war over Gibraltar.

Florida first came up in the negotiations in the issue of the Yazoo Strip, and the Strip continued a matter of discussion all through the talks. It had some of the small Mississippi River forts which Gálvez conquered in 1779 before he took Mobile and Pensacola. Before 1763 it had not been part of Spanish Florida but a part of the vast southern Indian area which was in dispute, claimed by Georgia as its western land and by Spain which had never really recognized the establishment of Georgia. After the

French-Indian War, the area was behind the English demarcation line of 1763, as Indian territory under English protection but off limits for American settlers. Now the Spanish reestablished claim to this southern Indian territory, all the way to the Ohio River. The French were also interested in it; and so it was that England, Spain, and even France claimed some sovereignty or protectorship of the Indian area and the Americans wanted it as part of the new United States. Professor Whitaker identifies the Yazoo Strip as the "heart of the Southern Indian country." Furthermore, the issue of free or closed navigation of the Mississippi River was intimately bound with the Strip and the southwest corner of Western Florida.

At one point, the American negotiator, John Jay, expressed the opinion that West Florida ought to revert to England. The Americans felt that England might be a counterbalance to Spain's total domination of the lower Mississippi if they, themselves, could not get possession of the east bank of the river to the thirty-first parallel or to 32′ 28' (the most northern point of the Yazoo Strip). This was a realistic outlook by Jay. He kept this position, but without much vehemence. Everything dealing with the Indian territory and with Florida was flexible.

The result of all this was the inclusion into the preliminary treaty of November 1782 between the Americans and the English of a secret West Florida clause dealing with the Strip. The "separate secret article" read that if West Florida became English again it would include the Yazoo Strip, but that if it remained Spanish the border would be the thirty-first parallel. This meant then that the Americans would receive the Strip, which included those Mississippi forts that were later to become Natchez and Vicksburg. The secret clause meant by implication that the Spanish occupation from Pensacola (in reality the Perdido River, about twenty miles west of Pensacola) to the Mississippi below the thirty-first parallel, not held by Spain previous to 1763, was sanctioned by the English and Americans. The western extension of Florida included places like Mobile, Biloxi, and Baton Rouge, part of French Louisiana previous to 1763.

Basically, this preliminary treaty became the permanent peace treaty. Since Spain kept both Floridas, the secret article of the preliminary treaty between England and the Americans became ineffective. But later, Spain, aware of the secret clause, refused to surrender the Strip, and the matter was not settled until the San Lorenzo Treaty, also called the Pickney Treaty of 1795, granted free navigation of the Mississippi River to the Americans and also settled the borders of Spanish West Florida, giving

Florida During the American Revolutionary War   [119]

the Strip to the United States. This area acquired under the Pickney Treaty, with lands north of it to the Tennessee River—part of the old southern Indian territory, became later the Mississippi territory. There have been "common assumptions by Americans in later years" that the real purpose of the secret clause was an attempt by the English "to embroil Spain and the United States." Professor Whitaker says, "No conclusive evidence has yet been produced to prove this," but that "circumstances certainly indicate that it was."

Naturally, with communications extremely slow and difficult, the inhabitants, newcomers and old timers alike, were nervous, and all kinds of rumors came and went. No one, including Governor Tonyn, knew what was happening at the peace negotiations. Under these circumstances it was difficult to maintain calm; St. Augustine and its surroundings never witnessed so much confusion, crime, and immorality as in 1782 and early 1783. By spring of 1783 the worst expectations became confirmed. News arrived of the return of East Florida to Spain. On April 21, the English governor officially announced the change and asked the non-Indian inhabitants to get ready for evacuation.

Soon afterward, however, rumors arrived that the English had decided to return Gibraltar to Spain in return for permanent possession of the two Floridas and Puerto Rico. People were joyous, and this was further enhanced when it became obvious that the final peace treaty had not yet been signed. Tonyn postponed his order. By the fall things looked gloomy again. The English military authorities discharged most of the troops stationed in St. Augustine, and other units left for Nova Scotia and the Bahamas. By November, one hundred-fifty men of the 37th Regiment arrived from New York, supposedly for ceremonial duties in the transfer procedures from English to Spanish hands. There was still hope in the minds of the inhabitants. By October no news of the final treaty had arrived. No one knew anything: would the Spanish arrive suddenly or would the Gibraltar deal go through?

Sometime in the spring of 1784, Tonyn received precise news which contained the definite peace terms of September 1783. He was ordered to evacuate the non-Indian population and deliver East Florida to the Spanish. He was given eighteen months for the sale of property and the removal of the to-be-evacuated population. Ships from Jamaica were promised for the evacuation and also land in the Bahamas for resettlement.

On May 6, 1784, Tonyn passed the news on to the population. All hope had now vanished. By June 27 the new Spanish governor, Manuel Zéspedes, arrived. On July 12, Tonyn delivered East Florida to Zéspedes, who, two days later, issued a proclamation declaring Spanish sovereignth and, with it, Spanish law over East Florida. Zéspedes reaffirmed the eighteen-month limit for the evacuation and liquidation of the English property and interests. But Tonyn requested that February 20, 1785, should be the target date for the total evacuation instead of March 19. Neither date could be kept and the Spanish graciously extended the deadline to July 19. Certainly, by April, nearly everyone had left. Tonyn stayed on beyond July and finally boarded ship in August, but continuous bad weather forced him to remain until November.

It was in this month of November 1785 that British rule came to an end in the Floridas. About seven hundred-fifty inhabitants remained and, of these, two-thirds were Catholic, non-Spanish Mediterraneans who had settled in Florida during the English period. A few English loyalists such as John Leslie, William Panton, and Jesse Fish remained to assume importance during the new Spanish rule. This second Spanish period would have to face a young and aggressive United States which felt that its new destiny included acquisition of East and West Florida.

BIBLIOGRAPHY

Bailey, Thomas A. *A Diplomatic History of the American People*. Several editions.
Bartram, William. *The Travels of William Bartram*. Edited by Mark Van Doren, with an introduction by John Livingston Lowes. 1940.
Bemis, Samuel Flagg. "Communications." *Hispanic American Historical Review* 7 (1927): 386-389.
_____. *The Diplomacy of the American Revolution*. Many editions and printings.
_____. *Pinckney's Treaty*. 1926, 1960.
Bennett, Charles E. *Southernmost Battlefields of the Revolution*. 1970.
Boyd, Mark and José Navarro Latorre. "Spanish Interest in British Florida, and in the Progress of the American Revolution." *Florida Historical Quarterly* 32 (1953): 92-130.
Carter, Clarence E. "The Beginnings of British West Florida." *Mississippi Valley Historical Review* 4 (1917): 314-341.
_____. "Some Aspects of British Administration in West Florida." *Mississippi Valley Historical Review* 1 (1914): 364-375.
Caruso, John Anthony. *The Southern Frontier*. 1963.
Caughley, John Walton. *Bernardo de Gálvez in Louisiana, 1776-1783*. 1934.

_____. "The Panis Mission to Pensacola." *Hispanic American Historical Review* 10 (1930): 480-489.

_____. "Willing's Expedition down the Mississippi, 1778." *Louisiana Historical Quarterly* 15 (1932): 5-36.

Doniol, Henri. *Histoire de la participation de la France a l'établissement des Etats-Unis d'Amérique*, 5 vols. 1886-1892.

Gipson, Lawrence Henry. "East Florida as a British Province, 1763-1765," in his *The Triumphant Empire*. Vol. 9. 1956.

_____. "The Empire on the Fringe of the Storm: East Florida, West Florida, 1770-1776," in *The Triumphant Empire*. Vol. 8. 1967.

_____. "West Forida as a British Province." in *The Triumphant Empire*. Vol. 9. 1956.

Gold, Robert L. *Borderland Empires in Transition*. 1969.

Haarmann, Albert W. "The Spanish Conquest of British West Florida, 1779-1781." *Florida Historical Quarterly* 39 (1960): 107-134.

Handlin, Oscar, et al. *Harvard Guide to American History*. 1963.

[Hanna] Abbey, Kathryn. "Efforts of Spain to Maintain Sources of Information in the British Colonies before 1779." *Mississippi Valley Historical Review* 15 (1928): 56-68.

Hanna, K. T. A. "The Place of the Floridas in the American Revolution." Typewritten article. Gainesville, Fla.: P. K. Yonge Library of Florida History, University of Florida. 1941.

[Hanna] Abbey, Kathryn Trimmer. "Spanish Projects for the Reoccupation of the Floridas during the American Revolution." *Hispanic American Historical Review* 9 (1929): 265-285.

Hanna, Kathryn Trimmer Abbey. *Florida, Land of Change*. 1941.

Harris, Michael H., compiler. *Florida History: a Bibliography*. 1972.

Holmes, Jack D. L. "Gálvez and the American Revolution," in his *Honor and Fidelity*. 1965.

_____. "A Spanish Province, 1779-1798," in *A History of Mississippi*, edited by Richard Aubrey McLemore. 1973.

Howard, Clinton N. *The British Development of West Florida, 1763-1769*. 1947.

_____. "Governor Johnstone in West Florida." *Florida Historical Quarterly* 17 (1939): 281-303.

_____. "The Military Occupation of British West Florida, 1763." *Florida Historical Quarterly* 17 (1939): 181-199.

Johnson, Cecil. *British West Florida, 1763-1783*. 1943.

_____. "Pensacola in the British Period: Summary and Significance." *Florida Historical Quarterly* 37 (1959): 263-280.

Konetzke, R. *Die Politik des Grafen Aranda*. 1929.

Kynerd, Byrle A. "British West Florida." in *History of Mississippi*, edited by McLemore. *Op. cit.*

Library of Congress. *The American Revolution: A Selected Reading List*. 1968.

Manucy, Albert, and Alberta Johnson. "Castle St. Mark and the Patriots of the Revolution." *Florida Historical Quarterly* 21 (1942): 3-24.

McAlister, L. N. "Pensacola during the Second Spanish Period." *Florida Historical Quarterly* 37 (1959): 281-325.

Morison, Samuel Eliot, and Henry Steele Commager. *The Growth of the American Republic*. Vol. 1. Several editions.

Mowat, Charles Loch. *East Florida as a British Province, 1763-1784.* 1943, 1964.

Nuceté-Sardi, José. *Aventura y tragedia de don Francisco Miranda*, 2d ed. 1935.

Pennington, Edgar Legare. "East Florida in the American Revolution, 1775-1778." *Florida Historical Quarterly* 9 (1930): 24-46.

Pérez Cabrera, José Manuel. *Miranda en Cuba (1780-1783).* 1950.

Rush, Orwin N. *The Battle of Pensacola, March 9 to May 8, 1781: Spain's Final Triumph over Great Britain in the Gulf of Mexico.* 1966.

Seibert, Wilbur H. *Loyalists in East Florida, 1774-1785: The Most Important Documents Pertaining thereto ... with an Accompanying Narrative*, 2 vols. 1929.

Taylor, Garland. "Colonial Settlement and Early Revolutionary Activity in West Florida up to 1779." *Mississippi Valley Historical Review* 22 (1935): 351-360.

Thorning, Joseph F. *Miranda: World Citizen.* 1952.

Whitaker, Arthur Preston. *The Spanish American Frontier.* 1927, 1962.

Worcester, Donald E. "Miranda's Diary of the Siege of Pensacola, 1781." *Florida Historical Quarterly*, 29 (1951): 163-196.

Yela Utrilla, J. F. *España ante la independencia de los Estados Unidos*, 2 vols., 2d ed. 1925.

Zapatero, Juan Manuel. *La Guerra del Caribe en el siglo XVIII.* 1964.

JOSE MARTI AND THE AMERICAN FOUNDING FATHERS
by Carlos Ripoll

Strident partisanship has in recent years brought to the fore those writings in which Martí portrayed the defects and errors of the United States he knew. His harsh indictments of the sectors of this nation debased by arrogance and the abuse of power are quoted often and with unwholesome satisfaction. In this oblique campaign to chastise the guilty, the accusers would obscure that Martí's anger was aroused rather by the guilt itself; for Martí, wrong was universally to be censured and deplored, and his words were ultimately intended to instill and encourage the principles and practice of human decency. What Martí abhorred in this country is quintessential today in some adversaries of this country: nothing here did he criticize more severely than the assault on liberty and justice.

Martí admired this nation which "with imperturbable generosity opened its arms...to the unfortunate and industrious of the earth," but he did not love it; his love went out to the South, to the peoples who compose what he piously called Mother America. He saw the hopeful looks cast north by the inexperienced republics in search of guidance, and he feared, correctly, that imitation would lead them astray, and that awe would lay open their frontiers to the greed of the very country at which they marveled. And so he used no reserve in uncovering to them "the truth about the United States," and in insisting to them that, "through its vices, through its mistakes, through its failings, it is necessary to study this country, so as not to fail or clash with it."

Exiled because of his activities in favor of Cuban independence, Martí arrived in New York for the first time at the beginning of 1875. He was twenty-two years old. Eleven years earlier, Spanish officials had sentenced him to hard labor and then banished him from Cuba; then, in Spain he studied at and graduated from the University of Saragossa, whereupon he fled to Mexico, stopping briefly in New York. In Mexico, he worked as a journalist until, chagrined at the excesses of those in power, he left for Guatemala, where he began a career as a teacher, only to abandon this country too, shortly after, for similar reasons. It was his second expulsion from Cuba that again brought Martí to the United States, in 1880; here he lived until 1895 carrying on the struggle to which he had dedicated his life and which led him to his death on May 19 of that year, at the outset of the independence war he had organized. His first employment in New York was as a journalist, and in some of the earliest articles he wrote for *The Hour,* a magazine devoted to the arts and letters, he left his impressions as a newcomer who had only recently ended years of instability and wanderings: "I am, at last, in a country where everyone looks like his own master. One can breathe freely, freedom being here the foundation, the shield, the essence of life."

Like no other Hispanic writer of this time, during his fifteen years in this country, Martí came to know and understand the ways and complex problems of United States society: the difficulties and the promise created by immigration; the racial prejudice; the burgeoning labor movement; the corruption in politics. For the newspapers of Central and South America he wrote magnificent chronicles on these and other topics as well as portraits of great Americans: Emerson, Whitman, Longfellow; Courtlandt Palmer—the "millionaire socialist"—, Henry Garnet—the black orator "who hated hate"—, Peter Cooper—"the friend of Man"—, Wendell Phillips—"the ardent knight of human dignity." Martí described the important events he witnessed and everything that in some way could contribute to an accurate and vivid image of the United States, the country that inspired in him both admiration and anxiety. "We love the land of Lincoln, just as we fear the land of Cutting," he said, summarizing his attitude; in the "sublime offspring of the lowly," he found the embodiment of nobility; in the "shameless reporter and adventurer" who maligned Mexico, the embodiment of conceit and malice.

When Martí took pen in hand, it was to enhance his subject, especially when the subject itself was adorned by virtue; and when he wrote in censure, it was with compassion and the sole purpose of bettering the world—never with hate, for few have been so apprehensive as he of that passion he called a poison and a crime. He held at his fingertips every device language and literature offered, and when these were insufficient, he created new and surprising ones, through sheer genius and without the slightest hint of effort or fatigue. And so, through his art were revealed to Spanish America myriad pictures of the United States as a land where the people performed feats worthy of giants but in their hurry seemed a swarm of ants; and through his insight was captured the nation's spirit in the strength of a hero or the smile of a child. The aged Domingo F. Sarmiento, who at the peak of his fame had Martí's "North American Scenes" read to him so that he could savour their inexhaustible expressive wealth, said: "In Spanish, there is nothing that compares with the swell and roar of Martí's prose, nor has anything comparable to his metallic resonance come out of France since Victor Hugo."

While totalitarian regimes are continually making Martí's works available to their people in their native tongues, falsifying through hushed censorship and abridgement the meaning and intent with which they were written, only a handful of Martí's works has been translated into English. The integrity of the texts must be restored and their translation encouraged; as Emil Ludwig has said, were they accessible to readers throughout the world, "they alone would suffice to make of Martí a source of leadership and guidance for our times." For the United States, Martí's writings have the added significance of providing, through an astute outsider's eyes, a critique of past errors and still-ingrained flaws, and a reminder of the treasures that must be appreciated and safeguarded. In the bicentennial of this nation's birth, it is most fitting that Martí's words inspire American readers to take stock of their shortcomings and their blessings.

"THE APOSTLES OF PHILADELPHIA"

Martí engraved in his memory every turn that history made, and he applied its lessons to the plight of Cuba. His first printed words about the revolutionary period were written in Mexico during the centennial of the Declaration of Independence. There, news reached him of the celebrations in New York, where many of his compatriots lived, like him refugees from Spanish tyranny. On July 4, they marched with the Cuban flag, and their gesture was hailed by sympathetic American observers. Martí took note of the occurrence in an article for the *Revista Universal:* "As the symbol of the heroic Antillean island was carried on the long parade, it was greeted not with applause, but with ovations. Does the blood shed valiantly by a people seeking freedom deserve less from a sister nation than cheers of affection and love? What nation, itself the offspring of oppression, is not moved and made proud by the exalted emblem of an energetic and revered people in whose glory are mirrored its own past glories?"

In the United States Martí found the cradle of liberty in the Americas, so he set himself to studying it; he inquired how and why the throne of freedom had been built and secured here, for he wanted to enthrone freedom in his native land. "Freedom is the Mother of the earth," "the essence of life," "the definitive religion," he said, and he sought to understand the progeny, the doctrines, and the rituals that made freedom flourish. But beside it, he found slavery: "In 1620 the Mayflower carried the pilgrims to Plymouth, and in 1620 a Dutch ship carried twenty African slaves to Virginia"; and so he was careful in his analysis to separate the two seeds, to set apart the Declaration of Independence from the federal Constitution. The former was for Martí "the genuine expression of the lofty spirit that moved the heroes and the preachers of liberty, that did battle in Bunker Hill and triumphed in Yorktown." But in the pacts of 1787 among the states, along with the precepts to ensure liberty, he saw guaranteed the iniquitous institution of bondage.

In his evocations of the revolutionary period, Martí captured the excitement awakened by Thomas Paine's *Common Sense* and the animation created in Philadelphia by the arrival of the delegates to the Second Continental Congress, from Pennsylvania, Virginia, the Carolinas, New York, and the rest of the thirteen colonies. He portrayed with equal measures of humanity and immortality the outstanding figures of the moment. Franklin was the "humble man," the "austere ambassador" to the French court "who entered the king's palace dressed in the modest garb of democracy, and spoke and triumphed with the language of liberty." He described Jefferson, "who had sworn eternal hostility to all forms of slavery," drawing up the draft of the Declaration, his tiny script "that of a soul contracted in its labors to strike in the hearts of men, like a flagstaff in its base, the ideas with which nations should be formed." And he drew attention to the very words so carefully chosen to convey those principles: "We hold these truths to be self-evident: that all men are created equal, that they are endowed by their Creator with certain inalienable rights, that among these are life, liberty, and the pursuit of happiness." Never before had such brilliant thoughts been pronounced upon the foundation of government among men; as Samuel Eliot Morison has rightly said, "These words are more revolutionary than anything written by Robespierre, Marx, or Lenin, more explosive than the atom, a continual challenge to ourselves, as well as an inspiration to the oppressed of all the world."

Martí studied the Constitution through the two-volume *History* by George Bancroft, whom he admired as an historian but reproached as the Secretary of the Navy under whose administration California was taken from Mexico. In an article he wrote for the Buenos Aires newspaper *La Nación* in 1877, Martí borrowed from Bancroft's account to render his own of the lively debates at the Convention and of the conflicting interests that had to be reconciled for the federation to be formed: the South's differences with the North, the farmers' with the industrialists, the big states' with the small, the slave states' with the free. And with a few details he characterized the delegates: Hamilton, "the impetuous aristocrat"; Madison, "precise and forthright," learned in letters and a scholar of history"; Gouverneur Morris, "a graduate from Kings College" and "creator of felicitous phrases"; William Paterson, of New Jersey, "a firm advocate of states' rights"; and Edmund Randolph, "the dramatic and attractive" Virginian "who defended centralism" and was "quicker to declaim than to think"; Nathaniel Gorham, the wealthy businessman who was "a choleric enemy of slavery"; James Wilson, "on whose arm Franklin leaned." But before all the founders Martí placed Washington. In him Martí saw incarnate the virtues that lent security to the American republic in its origins, and his praise was exuberant: Washington's steadfastness, his selflessness, his demeanor, all drew applause. Martí's Washington is more radiant after the hostilities ceased than before Newburgh, because he had learned in war the sobriety required to rule his countrymen. Fresh from his victories, he is described arriving at Philadelphia for the Convention, his path strewn with flowers by the women as he passed by; his most difficult battle was there: "The dissension Washington came to quiet was harsh at the time. The pernicious vociferators, the turbid spume that all revolutions arouse, appeared and took control, calling themselves progressive liberals. Others, preoccupied with instituting freedom, forgot to talk of freedom ... , and there were few heroes of the war whose ambitions for emoluments and sinecures did not tarnish their deeds."

Martí knew that a grandiose portrayal of the forging of the Constitution might cause in the reader a mistaken, idealized impression of the men who framed it. "Corn and beef speak the same tongue," he cautioned: "The fair-haired hates, deceives, and boasts the same as the dark-haired. The North-American becomes fanatic, angered, rebellious, confused, and corrupt just like the Spanish-American. One had only to witness the Convention! ... " Nevertheless, Martí, fair in his judgments, also knew that freedom presided over that contest; from the open and spontaneous arguments, he drew conclusions profitable to Spanish America: "That debate, natural in the political circumstances that produced it, was as fruitful as it was forceful. Sincerity is not to be feared; only what is kept hidden is tremendous. The public welfare requires the kind of combat that teaches respect; the kind of blaze that fires good ideas and consumes the useless ones; the kind of breeze that clears away the clouds, exposing in the light of day both the apostles and the rascals."

Martí has been criticized for not formulating a systematic body of doctrines, an outline for a constitution to direct the future of Cuba. His essays on the experience of Philadelphia reveal the reason for his silence: he understood a constitution to be "a living and practical law that cannot be structured with ideological components." The factors that might be comprised in the republic after independence had been won were unforseeable, and it would have been artificial and inopportune to try to build codes of law on thin air, anticipating the outcome. The Constitution of 1789, he said, "radiated the sunlight that, even with all the dark spots, seemed to Franklin the dawn." It was a compromise, a document that answered the specific needs of the nation and that should only be imitated if similar circumstances prevailed, and then not in the criminal concessions that blemished it. But despite its transigence with slavery, that document, in its vitality, proved what Martí proclaimed time and time again: "that only those forms of government that are native to nations take root in them." Still, following what he knew of the U.S. Constitution, with its failings and strengths, as well as what he knew of the failings and strengths the rest of the world had developed through a century of social and political ferment, he did clearly indicate in the program of the Cuban Revolutionary Party the route to follow once independence would be achieved: "to found on the free and honest exercise of the legitimate faculties of mankind a new and sincerely democratic people capable of overcoming, through authority sustained by real labors and by the equilibrium of the social forces, the dangers attendant upon sudden liberty in a society organized for slavery."

"The Statues of Porphyry"

Martí truly appreciated the merits of the founders of the United States when in 1884 he saw this country liberate itself from the rule of ineffectual and venal politicians of the Republican party through the exercise of the vote. The electoral fraud and arbitrary acts perpetrated by the government cast serious doubts on the system created in Philadelphia, but without disorder or bloodshed, the American people reclaimed its mandate from those who had betrayed it once in power. For Martí, the elections of that year were vindication and proof of the foresight and wisdom of the Convention of 1787. In the post-bellum era the Republican Party had decayed in its successive terms in high office, while its opposition had weakened; Martí perceived that "as victory rotted, it brought after it disintegration. The manifest of human freedom was turned into a shelter for money-changers." The same had happened earlier with the Democrats, he commented, as he described the period preceding the Civil War: "Freedom must be a constant practice else it degenerate into a banal formula. The very soil that produces a garden, produces nettles. All power widely and prolongedly held degenerates ... . The Democratic Party governed for so long in the past that the Constitution finally became in its hands a mere pile of wrinkled paper."

Living during that period of Republican control under which existed, as Martí said, an immoral consortium of "the magnates of politics" and "the potentates of the banks," he decried the situation: "The vehicle of suffrage was rolling on golden axles." There was also administrative irresponsibility: "Sure of their governmental machinery, and confusing the honest clamor of a tired nation with the shouting of a hungry people, the politicians reached shoulder deep into the coffers and foolishly squandered the treasury, even the huge surplus, in plans of obscure origin."

He watched with interest as dissension grew within the party: the Mugwumps split with the stalwarts at the nominating convention over the Blaine-Logan slate. The former was accused of having used public office for personal gain and of having turned the United States' role as mediator in the War of the Pacific to favor his friends and supporters. Martí was repulsed by the intrigues and unscrupulous maneuvers associated with Blaine and by his imperialist leanings; he was the leader of what Martí called *"ultraaguilismo"* ("ultra-eaglism") — the policy of "extending over much of the earth the wings of the American eagle." As Martí saw it, Blaine and his followers maintained that the Constitution was "a motheaten cape, a remnant from another time, and that an enterprising people needs roadways along which to expand, not a constable to tie its hands."

The Mugwumps, the rebellious Republicans who rejected the party ticket, were, in contrast, "listening to the solemn dictates of Webster, following the heroic spirit of the sacred apostles of Philadelphia"; they wanted "freedom—simple, respectful, magnanimous, and pure, and they repeated in the press and in their speeches clear, honest words that sounded like those of titans come to sit among men, as in the sublime days when Washington made the peace, Madison, plans, and Hamilton, provisions; Franklin counseled, Jefferson urged forward." The ideals and acts of the founding fathers were always Martí's yardstick in appraising the course of the nation and its leaders.

He was filled with enthusiasm by the popular reaction against corrupt and incompetent government and by the proper use of the franchise to channel that reaction:

> Anyone who observes this country without prejudice, no matter how much displeased by the priority it gives the appetites and by its slight, if not disdain, of generosity, must recognize that, with the regularity of a law, whenever it seems that danger to the nation is imminent, that one of its institutions is irremediably corrupted, or that vice has partly devoured it, the men and the systems through which the destruction can be avoided arise, without fanfare, and when the ills can still be cured.

During the campaign for the presidential election of 1884, such a man was Grover Cleveland, the Democratic candidate, who then appeared to Martí "a man of reason and integrity" and "the reformer that the times required." The reaction had become evident with the numerous Democratic victories in the midterm elections of 1882; Martí wrote of them early the following year: "What a splendid agitation in this country two or three months ago! It is like a sleeping giant that, certain of the strength it will need in time of trial, does not hasten to rise; but it does rise, it wields its enormous hammer, crushes the enemy or the obstacle in its way, and sleeps again. ... With the majestic and serene show of the magnificent force of peace, the people gave the nation's vote to the new men of the Democratic Party. The weary nation turned its back on the heroes and corrupt advisers. Ah!, it was grand; it made one rejoice in belonging to the human race." Then he described the Democrats who called for reform and change as indignant apostles "brandishing like swords in the face of the vote sellers the texts of Jefferson, Madison, and Jackson...."

In the national election, Martí's hopes that the Republicans would be defeated were fulfilled: Blaine was beaten by Cleveland. Martí mused over the event, which he interpreted idealistically as a sign of moral rebirth for the country:

> Just when the political institutions, in their application, and human nature appeared corrupt, as they are in older nations; when after only a century Washington's wig was mere dust, Franklin's waistcoat, motheaten, and Jefferson's figure, leperous decay; when one beheld in the spirit of government insolence, usurpation, and impulse to seize control in and outside the land, under cloak of freedom but contrary to its essence..., out of their silence came the vigilant thinkers, who are, like the marrow of the human body, the hidden essence of their peoples; and the Republic showed itself superior to the danger it faced.

Martí asked himself where that strength came from, that marvelous power to rescue from spurious leaders the government of the nation, and to dissolve the immoral pact of government and selfish interests that prospered in democracy's shadow. Inspired by the events he had witnessed, he discerned the answer in the organization of the country provided for by the Declaration of Independence and the Constitution, which gave safe refuge to the law and, more than a century after they had been penned, guaranteed the rights and liberties their authors had fought to secure. Nothing Martí wrote in praise of the United States is more fervent or eloquent than this passage he devoted to the memory of the founding fathers when he saw in the Democratic triumph that of the system, and in Cleveland's victory, that of America's apostles of Philadelphia:

> I would sculpt in porphyry the statues of the extraordinary men who forged the Constitution of the United States of America; I would sculpt them in porphyry in a group as they signed their prodigious work. I would lay a sacred road of unpolished marble blocks leading to a temple of white marble that would guard their remains; and I would declare a week of national pilgrimage every few years, in the autumn, the season of maturity and beauty, so that the reverent—the men, women, and children, their heads enveloped in the fragrant clouds of dry leaves—might go to kiss the hand of stone of the patriarchs. I am not dazzled by great size. I am not dazzled by wealth. The material prosperity of a free people does not dazzle me.... Neither men, nor novelties, nor brilliant acts of daring, nor colossal crowds dazzle me. But when one sees this majesty of the vote, this new nobility of which every man is a member, be he obstreperous pauper or owner of gold, this monarch of a multitude of faces, that cannot want to do itself harm, because it is only as great as its domain, which is itself; when one witnesses this unanimous exercise of will by ten million men, one feels as if he were mounted on a steed of light and goading its winged hooves, as if leaving behind an old world in ruins to pass through the gates of a universe of dignity, at the threshold of which a woman beside an open ballot-box cleanses the muddied or beaten brow of those who enter. The ones who lifted and raised on high with serene

hands to that new universe the sun of decorum; the ones who sat down to make reins of silk for mankind, and made them, and gave them to man; the ones who bettered man, those are the ones I would sculpt in statues of porphyry for a temple of marble. And I would pave so all might go pay them homage a road of marble, wide and white.

THE CULTURAL PRESENCE OF THE CUBAN EXILE IN MIAMI
*by Rosa M. Abella**

Cuba seems to be a country destined to the forced displacement of its inhabitants. Its first settlers were Indians that came from Venezuela and Florida. They lived in a calm, primitive environment until the coming of other groups, the Tainos, indigenous to the Lesser Antilles. These people, with a more advanced civilization, dominated the first inhabitants, who had to seek refuge in the western portion of Cuba. Less than a century before Columbus' arrival other more culturally advanced groups penetrated the Baracoa region, and forced the peaceful Ciboneys back to the central areas of the Island. If there would have been no discovery, even the latest arrivals would have been driven out by new invaders, the Caribs, who were already on the Tainos' tracks.

Spain's pressure at the beginning of the conquest was so intense that before the end of the sixteenth century the disappearance of the Indians forced the Crown to import black slaves. The violence of slavery created a new imbalance in the population of the Island, with the deserting slaves forming new groups of refugees in mountainous areas. Those black *cimarrones,* locked in their stockades, in places inaccessible to the dogs and the trackers that were following them, are another example of the displacements in the country, product of force and abuse.

Every segment of society that isolates itself from the main nucleus does this obeying the instinct of self-preservation before inmediate danger of its life or, slowly and surely, when the environment is hostile to survival.

*Translated by Margaret Khuly.

Cuba, in the first years of the conquest, lacked the gold that the Spanish were looking for, and because of this became poorer as time went by. That is why the ostracism of those who directed themselves towards *Tierra Firme* (the Mainland; specifically Mexico) started; and emigration reached such extremes that those who tried to leave the Island were punished with the death penalty. Then came two centuries of being victimized by pirates and filibusterers, a stable population lacking. Later, with the development of the sugar industry resulting in a source of riches for the Spaniards, the importation of slaves increased. With a greater number of black slaves in the Island and more abuses committed, charitable voices were raised against the injustices perpetrated. Before the end of the seventeenth century authorities sent into exile two Capuchin friars that declared themselves against slavery in Havana. Maybe in them we find the precursors of the political exiles from Cuba.

As the differences between the Spanish and the *criollos* or Creoles became stronger, it also became harder to live together, and conspiracy against the mother country started, following the example of the North American English colonies and the various uprisings in South America. Hope for political improvement on the Island disappeared, and the Cubans were frustrated by the negative attitude of the Spanish government concerning the deputies to the courts of Cádiz. Their most important figure, the priest Félix Varela, would head the vast list of Cubans to seek refuge in the United States. Varela, after living in New York and Philadelphia and working against the Spanish Crown—protected by the freedom offered by the United States, went to live at St. Augustine in Florida. He died there in 1853, being without doubt the first Cuban, the most exemplary and eminent, that perished far from his homeland because of the intolerance of the colonial government.

As a consequence of the defeat of Spain in the continent, new conspiracies broke out, and the Cubans suffered greater persecutions. In 1823, José María Heredia had to follow Varela and leave his country. Here, in the United States, he heard he had been sentenced to permanent exile. Not being able to withstand the rigors of the cold weather, he left to reside in Mexico, where he died. Martí could only find one mistake in Heredia's life: his return to Cuba to visit his mother and his palm trees.

José Antonio Saco was another of the great expatriates of the nineteenth century. He raised his voice before those who wanted to end

The Cultural Presence of the Cuban Exile in Miami

the recently inaugurated Academia Cubana de Literatura (Cuban Academy of Literature); under such pretext he was punished for his attacks on slavery. He left Cuba and died in exile in 1879.

Varela, Heredia, and Saco headed the banishment, and they were followed by other names that enrich Cuba's national history: Aguilera, Morales Lemus, Aldama, Villaverde, Zenea, Martí, Maceo, and more.

From Narciso Lopez' first expeditions until independence was obtained in 1898, different nuclei started coming into existence in different parts of the continent, but mostly along the southern coast of the United States; and, particularly, after the start of the *Guerra Grande* (1868-1878), in Key West, Tampa, and other cities in Florida. The Cubans immigrating to the United States always appreciated the generousity and sympathy of the North Americans, but they never gave up their customs and traditions. Because of that they founded schools to educate their children, clubs for mutual support, patriotic organizations to recall the past, and other cultural groups.

It seemed that with the establishment of the Cuban Republic the periods of exile would have ended for the Cubans. Yet, three decades did not go by until Gerardo Machado's persecutions began to be felt. This time Miami became the center of the immigration: students, workers, military men, businessmen, and professionals found, from 1931 on, refuge in certain sectors of this city that years later would come to be known as "Little Havana." The government of Fulgencio Batista afterwards brought on a new wave of exiles. With Castro's imposition and the establishment of a Communist tyranny, one-tenth of the Cuban population left the Island, while hundreds of thousands—millions—are trapped by a government afraid of national depopulation.

Pushed by a self-preservation instinct, the first to leave Cuba were those attached to Batista's regime. They numbered some three thousand. Later, revolutionary laws forced out from the Island many that were against the new system. The expatriates of 1959 believed that the exile was going to be short. With the thwarted invasion of the Bay of Pigs in 1961, the situation changed. Great groups of Cubans realized that it was impossible to live freely in Cuba. And so, first on commercial airline flights, then on special flights provided by the government of the United States, and on improvised rafts and boats, heroically facing the dangers of the Straits of Florida, 800,000 or more left. Of these, hundreds did not arrive, dying by drowning or devoured by sharks. Meanwhile, the exile community became more heterogeneous, with all strata of society united by love of freedom and alarm at losing their own spiritual character.

But, what happens to a city like Miami when in less than fifteen years a foreign population arrives, estimated in 1974 at 400,000 and comprising half of its inhabitants — a quarter of the population of Dade County? Today, the conditions in "Little Havana" are not the same as in 1931, 1952, or 1957 when the presence of Cubans passed without notice. Now Miami feels the contact with another language, with refugees who have tried not to give up their national heritage and who, at the same time, revitalize and exalt it.

In his desire to be linked to Cuba, and faced with the reality of an exile longer than expected, the Cuban recreates in the city of Miami many of his institutions, trying to preserve and pass on to his children his traditions and customs. The exile of the decade of the sixties and beginnings of the seventies embraces his beliefs and is afraid that because of lack of care or outside influences, he may lose the ties with his island. As his ancestor of the nineteenth century, he organized schools to educate his children, benevolent associations, and cultural institutions patterned after his own character. The presence of so many representative of diverse social and economic classes, and of different cultural levels, causes a notable impact on Miami. The Spanish language, heard on the streets, in the schools, in the churches, the theaters, the hospitals, and the prisons, changes the former profile of the place. Today, Miami has a cultural environment that includes artistic aspirations very similar to those existing in any urban center of Hispanic America.

The purpose of this chapter is to relate some of these efforts.

Faced by an unexpected outpour of Cuban children arriving without their parents and with no knowledge of the English language, the school system of Dade County was caught at a disadvantage. At the beginning of the decade of the sixties, ways to solve this serious and urgent problem were generously created. The magnanimous solution reached at that time was to declare Miami a bilingual city by the beginning of 1970. An example of the official role the Spanish language would assume in Florida was the order to print electoral ballots both in English and in the language of the newly arrived.

The theater, that other vital means to communicate a language, made its appearance in "Little Havana" in the first years of exile. A lot has happened in scenic art from the opening of *Añorada Cuba* to the successes of groups of performers and directors today. The theater Las Máscaras, founded in 1968 at a small commercial locale on Eighth Street, today occupies a building designed exclusively for its shows and has an enthusiastic following. The road from *La luz que agoniza*, some years ago, to *Sé infiel y no mires con quién*, viewed by 18,000 persons, shows the tenacity that leads to achievement. On the billboards of the Sala Teatro Carrusel the best-known writers of Cuban drama have appeared, and their plays have been directed by prestigious figures of the Cuban theater.

In non-professional theater we have to signalize the work of Miami Dade Community College, conscious of the duty of theatrical literature in society. It has presented al fresco a good Spanish repertoire, and its *Cucarachita Martina*, offered both in English and Spanish for children, was a success. For years Sociedad Pro-Arte Gratelli has been producing a monthly show. The best Spanish *zarzuelas* and classical pieces of lyrical Cuban theater and of a universal repertoire have been presented with great success by the Sociedad in Dade County Auditorium: Federico Moreno Torroba was present at the festival of his own *zarzuelas;* and an operetta of Gonzalo Roig, *Cecilia Valdés*, in which the Spanish actress Nati Mistral had the leading role, was highly acclaimed by the Spanish-speaking audience which filled the auditorium in 1974.

The Sociedad Artístico Cultural de las Américas is an institution created to stimulate and encourage musical art in the Hispanic community. The Sociedad brought to Gusman Hall, *Cuba: dos siglos de música* (Cuba: Two Centuries of Music). *Ballet Concerto*, established since 1965, might be the artistic expression patronized by Cubans that has reached the American public the most because of the special attribute of universality that the choreography has. Besides exiled dancers, it has brought international figures such as Natalia Makarova and Ivan Nagy.

Cuban immigrants to Miami have created and maintained art galleries with periodic exhibitions. Bacardí Art Gallery offers almost every two weeks exhibits of Cuban painters and sculptors and of artists of other nationalities. The prestige of this gallery and its programs has been reflected in the North American press. The same type of activity has taken place in Galerie 4, which also has organized talks about the plastic arts. De Quirós Lesver Art Gallery and the Old Curiosity Shop, both also directed by Cubans, maintain regular exhibits. On the other hand, Miami can also boast of having one of the smallest art galleries in the world—its Mini Gallery, which measures forty-six inches wide by twenty-nine feet long. Its location facilitates its being viewed by a numerous public, and it is a recommended sight-seeing place for tourists visiting the city. Because of such cultural interest, the great exhibit of "Pintura Cubana" ("Cuban Painting") in the Miami Art Center was also possible. With panoramic vision, canvases covering a period of two hundred years were exhibited, from Nicolás de la Escalera and Vicente Escobar, at the end of the eighteenth century and beginnings of the nineteenth, up to established artists in our day.

In 1968, a small group of Cuban women got together and organized what is today the Cuban Women's Club, with more than four hundred members. The club's affairs are principally cultural, altruistic, and civic.

The *Cruzada Educativa Cubana* (Cuban Educational Crusade), founded in 1962 by professional people, is characterized by its programs aimed at maintaining a Cuban tradition. It presently bestows the *Premio Juan J. Remos* (Juan J. Remos Prize). The *Cruzada* sponsors the *Círculo de Juventudes Ignacio Agramonte* (Ignacio Agramonte Youth Circle) to spread the study of Cuban history and preserve among the youth a love of the mother country.

The *Asociación Fraternal Latinoamericana* (the Fraternal Latin-American Association) was one of the first cultural associations in exile. Established in 1961, it started exhibits of exile paintings, and theater presentations with Cuban artists; today it keeps a library, and it held, in the years 1964 and 1965, the first exhibition of books written by Cuban immigrants.

There are several Cuban radio and television stations in Miami. Radio WQBA, *"La Cubanísima,"* with its typical love of exaggeration, stands out with WFAB, known as *"La Fabulosa"* (The Fabulous One). Cuban radio in Miami not only transmits news and Spanish programs, but it has participated in campaigns to help our community and that of other nations of the hemisphere. TV channel 23 transmits all its news programs and *novelas* ("soap operas") in Spanish. Channel 4, via radio, dubs into Spanish its 6 p.m. daily news program.

No single form of expression — other than live dialogue — is more plentiful among immigrants, of all times and all nationalities, than the written one. The bibliography of Cuban writers outside the Island is impressive. To satisfy the demand of Spanish readers, and to keep in touch with the production of Cuban writers, Miami has several bookstores, such as the Librería y Distribuidora Universal, which also publishes a catalog of Cuban titles, and the Librería Cervantes. The city of Miami has been considered so important in this field that the Instituto del Libro Español

(Institute of the Spanish Book) has recently opened an establishment here for the sale of works published in Spain.

Even more fertile has been the accomplishment of the press. It would be impossible to mention here even a small number of the newspapers and magazines printed in Miami. But few have survived the difficulties of such an enterprise. The University of Miami Library preserves a very rich collection of such an important production, with the expectation that in the future it will constitute a valuable source for investigation. Among the newspapers, *Diario Las Américas* stands out: its director, Dr. Horacio Aguirre, born in Nicaragua, made his the exiles' cause from the first day of the Cuban revolution, and the paper has become a vehicle of difusion of great reach. Numerous Cubans, Spaniards, and Hispanic Americans cooperate with Dr. Aguirre as columnists, correspondents, employees, and printers.

The preservation of our traditions and culture has been made possible by the schools directed by Cubans, where bilingual education has allowed the youths to retain their mother language. Belén Jesuit School, established in the center of "Little Havana," today has numerous students, and exercises its influence through Ramón Guiteras Public Library. Garcés Commercial College imparts a commercial bilingual education, and is very prestigious in the community as a whole. Conchita Espinosa Academy, Miami Aerospace Academy, La Salle School, Francisco Baldor School, Loyola School, and others have a distinguished student body of Hispanic Americans that participate not only in academic activities, but in civic and community affairs.

This brief enumeration of Cuban cultural manifestations in Miami should not leave out the *Cámara de Comercio Latina* (Latin Chamber of Commerce), an association of businessmen that started with seventeen members in 1965 and today has more than one thousand six hundred members. It was established to promote commercial initiative, but the scope of its work has surpassed the limits of its initial aim. The house where it is located has been opened for exhibits, conferences, and classes. The CAMACOL, as it is called, a product of the Cuban immigration, has loaned its facilities to civic and charitable associations, and on an inter-American level has given support to campaigns to aid Nicaragua, Guatemala, and Honduras when these were afflicted by great disasters.

The insular condition and mobility of Cuba's inhabitants have shaped the way of being a Cuban: may be from this comes a great virtue, the capacity for success; and a great fault, improvisation — both a result of adapting with urgency. And no place of refuge has received so deep an imprint as Dade County in Florida. It is true that no other region in the world has received such a great number of our compatriots, caused by an exile from Cuba that has lasted the longest of any, since no other political regime in the Island forced so many to such long expatriation. Because of this, the changes evidenced in the area are more remarkable and produce greater results than elsewhere, not only in day-to-day living — food, language, and recreation, but on the cultural level and in all intellectual enterprises, through which the grateful Cuban is each day permitted here in the United States to commit himself more deeply to his nationality and to his destiny.

Editor's Note: Some of the cultural contributions well-pointed out by Dr. Abella were accomplished with partial funds of U.S.A. foundations and, in some instances, by metropolitan Miami. In keeping with the spirit and the title of our book, other Hispanic contributions should be added. Even before the Cuban revolution the Drama Department of the University of Miami produced in its Ring Theater, both in Spanish and English, Casonas' play *La barca sin pescador,* and (in English) García Lorca's *Yerma* and *La casa de Bernarda Alba.* Spain has contributed to the Bicentennial celebrations by sending twice to our shores her school ship *Juan Sebastian de Elcano,* as well as an excellent collection of a few of her outstanding modern painters, including Sorolla, Mir, and Darío Regoyos, exhibited in July 1976 at the small Bacardi gallery in Miami.

A donation to Florida of a statue of Ponce de León has been already approved in Madrid. On different occasions, the greatest virtuoso of the guitar, Andrés Segovia, visited Dade County. Later on, Carlos Montoya came. Upon mentioning the master of *flamenco* music and so returning to concert programs, the name of Juan Mercadal, now so much a part of our community, is to be remembered.

To the Institute of Puerto Rican Culture we owe the presentation of *Areyto,* its official ballet corps with authentic, earthly roots, directed by Irene McLean, and the visit of the famous Figueroa Quintet—five brothers graduated from the Madrid Conservatory and from the Normal School of Music in Paris. Other Puerto Ricans—singers and actors—of the prestige of Justino Díaz, Raúl Dávila, Pablo Elvira, Emilio Belaval, Jr., and Antonio Barasorda have been heard among us.

We will not attempt to mention the considerable number of Spanish and Hispanic lecturers, authors, and painters that have stopped in our city: but, among the playwrights, the Spaniard Antonio Buero Vallejo must be noted; and among the recitalists, we wish to mention Rosita Ginorio from Puerto Rico, who has lived here for many years; and among the university professors, Dr. Juan J. Remos, who left an unforgettable memory in Miami.

CHARACTERISTICS AND CONSEQUENCES of the Hispanic Economy in Miami Before and After the Cuban Communist Revolution
by Antonio Jorge*

The principal objective of this chapter is to briefly describe and analyze the characteristics and consequences of the Hispanic economy in Miami, before and after the Communist revolution in Cuba in 1959.

The reader will observe in this chapter that the description and examination undertaken are, of necessity, limited. The reasons for this are as follows: In the first place, the data on the participation of Hispanic groups in the local economy prior to the arrival of the exiled Cubans in 1959 are too meager to offer a solid base upon which to arrive at conclusions as to their importance. In the second place, although there is a general consensus about the importance of the Cuban contribution and of the growing influence of other Hispanic groups, it would be difficult to postulate what course the local economy might have taken in the absence of the impact of this Hispanic population.

It is not difficult to cite some general figures which will indicate the weight of the Hispanic economy in relation to the total economy. Through labor data, together with the occupational distribution and educational level of the Hispanic population, we can get a valid picture of the nature of the economic activities being carried on by this segment of the community. Past tendencies and probable future economic development, as well as the structural changes brought about by them, allow us to speculate on the possible role the Hispanic population will have in Dade County. This is

---

*Translated by Piedad F. Robertson. Notice should also be taken of the dedicated work of Humberto Solís, an Economics doctoral student, who gathered data and evaluated information in a report which has been of great help in preparing this chapter.

especially easy to see, when, as in the present case, there are areas of growth which will be, by their nature, associated with the qualifications and aptitudes of the Hispanic population segment.

Necessarily we will have to make a hypothetical assumption in determining which of the alternative routes of local social-economical development would have materialized if the historic conditions which so unexpectedly brought about the massive arrival of Cubans in Dade County had been absent. There are good reasons which lead us to conclude that if this phenomenon had not occurred, the development of the area would have proceeded in a different manner.

Let us examine this factor more closely, for it is the only aspect of the problem to which suggestions and opinions can be offered which are relatively new. Let us concentrate first on the Cuban aspect, not only because it is numerically the most important, but also because it has certain singular characteristics not found in other situations which might have been similar.

First, there is a great deal of interdependence, apparent at first glance, in the Cuban market, especially in reference to the buying and selling of consumer goods and institutional, professional, and personal services of any kind. The relative segregation of this market would not have arisen if Dade County had continued growing in the customary manner of internal migration from different parts of the country.

One of the most important points, if not the fundamental one, in an in-depth investigation of the Hispanic economy, should be the measurement of the nature, reach, and degree of the sectoral interrelation in that market. Of equal importance are the choices with regard to the buying and selling of goods, given to the consumer. One could state *a priori* and with a considerable degree of accuracy, that higher coefficients of interdependence will be found among those links in the production chain that are closer to the consumer than anywhere else. This is easily seen in the Dade County economy, which is similar to the "open" economic systems. This means that the area depends largely on commercial relations with other national, as well as foreign markets. It has a very specialized economic structure that, although in the process of diversification, will always depend heavily on certain activities, most of which are in the service areas, public as well as private. This structure makes our local economy similar, though not in income, to the economies of underdeveloped areas.

It is possible that the distribution of the economic and financial investments of Cubans and Hispanic Americans in general have contributed to the growth of this zone, especially with regard to the development of the Hispanic market itself. This is so because the Hispanic economic activities have been molded by special conditions that oriented it toward the satisfaction of consumer needs. The reason for this is clear. The Cuban exiles are a vertical sampling of the population of the Cuban republic. The different professions, occupations, and skills complement each other, helping to form a tight interdependent network of goods and services. This interdependence helps not only to preserve the cultural characteristics and identity of the economic agents, but also by its very nature offers a mutual support in generating income and jobs amongst Hispanic peoples. This tendency of the Cuban exile has been reinforced by the increasing immigration from South and Central American countries.

It can be said that the development of the Hispanic economy has followed a pattern of balanced growth in the market. The different sectors of this economy have developed in a parallel manner, thus bringing about a horizontal integration of the Hispanic market. Vertical relationships have been slower to establish themselves because of the "open" characteristic of the local economy. These relationships are usually found in a market economy at a more advanced stage of development.

The Cuban contribution to local economy, without doubt, has certain unique aspects as a result of the situation faced by the exiles. Among these aspects, the most prominent one is the psychological factor. The exile feels himself to be in a critically insecure situation created by the abrupt social-economical changes with which he lives. This operates as a strong incentive to work and to produce. The "Fidelista" revolution has poured into Miami large numbers of people forced to acquire many of the characteristics of earlier dynamic minority immigrations: a minority that faces the risk of the new and the unknown. This phenomenon is far from new. It is amply documented in studies of economic development and social psychology.

As a result of this situation, imposed on them by circumstances in their homeland, the Cubans have displayed in the United States an attitude, with regard to economic activity, which is not typical of their culture. The competitive and vigorous behavior in the economic area is the product of an individualized and secularized cultural environment where empiric values rule absolute in the organization of activities. In this respect, it would be interesting to further investigate, by means of a psychological study on attitudes and motivations, the changes undergone by Cubans and other Hispanic-American people during the process of aculturation, even though it might be done only partially and limited initially to the economic world.

All these conditions make the Cubans, as well as the other Hispanic people who have decided to try their luck as immigrants in search of better opportunities, a good paradigm of the economic agent in the field of classical economy. The Hispanic-American demographic flow into this area served principally, in the decade of the sixties, to encourage competition. Through salary competitiveness, the resulting lowering of production costs, the greater personal effort, and the increment of productivity, this new segment of the population created a mechanism of economic growth which corresponds to the old pattern of the classical school of economy.

The Cuban case particularly deserves special study with respect to the causal mechanism of economic development in Dade County in the first years of the past decade. It is an example of growth foreign to the governing models in the economics of modern consumer societies. Here we have witnessed an initial growth in the volume of production and in income as a consequence of a primary expansion in the work force. This is a first-class example of the operation of the well-known Law of Say in which an increase in the supply can subsequently produce a corresponding increase in the demand.

The Hispanic-American economic activity in Miami has also served to imprint on the area a cosmopolitan characteristic which is a guarantee of sustained and stable future growth. The continuous expansion of tourism from the South; the international banks that proliferated in Miami under the protection of the Edge Act; the great number of international companies which have established here their principal offices for Hispanic-America; the rapid increase in the volume and value of the international cargo that comes through the port of Dodge Island and through the airport, as well as the development of Miami as an international center for commerce and light manufacture for exportation with the great possibilities for becoming a financial market for the republics to the South, indicate more accessible avenues of expansion in the years to come.

As to local commerce and tourism, domestic as well as Hispanic, it should be pointed out that the arrival of Cubans and Hispanic-American people in general, and their establishment in the center of the city and in the surrounding areas saved Miami from a decline common to other modern big cities. The zone commonly known as "Little Havana" is an extraordinary example of private urban renewal. From the standpoint of location of tourist services and commercial establishments, the revitalization of the city of Miami has been of great benefit privately as well as publicly.

One should also consider the fact that Hispanic Americans have created a closely knit market which is to a great degree self-supportive. This does not mean that the benefits derived reach only the other members of the Hispanic community. In the first place, as has been indicated, the degree of vertical integration of the economic sectors that make up the total market is not high. This is due to the nature and structure of the local economy as well as to the natural preferences and priorities with regard to the amount and distribution of the investments made by Hispanic investors. A notable exception to this has been the gradual expansion and growth of the agricultural, industrial, and transformational enterprises directed towards the production of goods of a generic character known by the Hispanic consumers or of other specific products that enjoy a special position because of the commercial brands associated with them. Another interesting case is the construction industry. Hispanic contractors have come to represent between forty percent and fifty percent of the economic net value of construction in Dade County. In order to maintain a correct perspective in viewing the situation, the fact should be emphasized that the Hispanic market has multiple and strong connections at all levels with the diverse markets in the area including the important markets of distribution and sale of consumer goods should be emphasized. It would not be correct to maintain a hypothesis based on the belief that these markets are watertight compartments completely separated from each other.

Finally, we could add to the list of specific contributions to local economy the investment in federal funds received in this zone as a result of the refugee Cuban population of school age in the educational system, and also the federal money from the refugee program. It should be noted that different researches have proven more than once that the above-mentioned educational and cultural-impact funds in reality subsidized the local system. Excluding the initial period of Cuban influx to Miami, school taxes were sufficient to cover the expenses undergone by the absorption of the Cuban children into the school system. The same reasoning may be applied as to the federal funds to help the refugees. This is why these funds, although technically appearing to transfer money to this zone, were in reality compensated for by the payment of local, state, and federal taxes.

Let us continue now with some brief remarks on the economic significance of the arrival in Dade County of a great number of Hispanic Americans basically during the last decade.

The 1970 census estimated the number of Cubans and Cuban descendants in the Miami area at approximately 218,000. In 1960, the number in that same area was 29,000. The total of Spanish-speaking persons in Dade County was 299,000 according to the 1970 census. Generally these estimates are considered quite low since there is a tendency to systematically sub-represent ethnic minorities, in this case Hispanic. Dependable estimates, such as J. Clark's ideas about population, give the number of Cubans in Dade County alone as having increased to 350,000 in 1972. In the case of the Cubans, there exists an element of calculation error. This is in regard to the number of people who, originally relocated in other areas of the country after their arrival, decided to return here on their own once it was financially possible to do so. Taking all this into consideration, it is possible that the Cuban population in Dade County constitutes 85 percent of the total Hispanic-American inhabitants in the area. Based on what has been said previously and by demographic information up to 1974, one can estimate the Cuban population in Dade to be 26 percent of the total. This is up from 3.1 percent in 1960 and 17.2 percent in 1970.

Overall population growth figures for Metropolitan Miami *(Standard Metropolitan Statistical Area of Miami)* during the past decades are, according to the Metropolitan Dade County Planning Department, as follows: an increase of 87 percent between 1930 and 1940; another 85 percent between 1940 and 1950; an 89 percent increase from 1950 to 1960; and finally, a 36 percent increase in the 1960 decade. It should be noted that about 70 percent of this final 36 percent were Cubans. The national average of increase for this last period was only 13 percent. The growth of Dade County from 1970 to 1974 was 19.2 percent, a rate surpassed only in Arizona. Provided no laws are passed to restrict growth, one can reasonably expect a compound rate of population increase of about 30 percent per decade between now and 1990.

The facts given on population can be correlated with figures on the growth of income for the area, especially during the previous decade.

Characteristics and Consequences [147]

According to figures from the *Survey of Current Business* published by the U.S. Department of Commerce for the years 1972 and 1973, the total personal income (shown) for the Standard Metropolitan Statistical Area of Miami, was $2,087 million in 1959, and $6,156 million in 1971. The average annual rate of growth of income was 9.43 percent between 1959 and 1971 and 10.97 percent between 1969 and 1971. The per capita income in the area increased from $2,299 in 1959 to $4,706 in 1971. For the nation as a whole, the per capita income in 1971 was $4,157. It should also be pointed out that Southern Florida as a whole reported a per capita income of $3,930 for 1971.

A further proof of the growing strength of the Metropolitan Dade County economy relative to 254 other similar areas in the country may be found in the publication, *Standard Metropolitan Statistical Area of Miami,* which reports a rise in personal income from the seventy-sixth position in 1959 to twenty-seventh in 1971. Another statistical index projects a continuing growth for the state of Florida, estimating an increase of 163 percent between 1969 and 1990.

If we concentrate solely on the income generated in the area, we see that in 1971 it was $4.869 billion. This figure represents an increase of approximately 23 percent compared to the 1969 figure which was $3.965 billion. One should notice that the increase of personal income of residents in comparison to that of persons that only work in the area is of $1.187 billion. This indicates that the transfer of net income to the area is considerable. An interesting fact about local economic growth is that in 1970, a recession year, the rate of increase was about 9 percent, the same as in 1971, which was a recovery period. According to the data given in the *Comprehensive Manpower Plan of the M.A.P.C. of Dade and Monroe Counties,* the economy of Southern Florida experienced an extraordinary growth of more than 20 percent during the period of economic expansion, 1971-1972. Manufacturing construction and tourism were the industries which contributed the most to this development.

In order to give an overall idea of the composition of the economic development in the Standard Metropolitan Statistical Area of Miami in recent years we have reproduced the following table of the sectional origin of local income.*

---

*Survey of Current Business Vol. 53, no. 5 (May 1973). Figures are in millions.

[148]　　　　　　　　　THE HISPANIC PRESENCE IN FLORIDA

	1969	1970	1971
1. Total income	$3,965	$4,453	$4,869
2. Agricultural income	47	40	50
3. Total income, not agricultural	3,919	4,413	4,820
4. Governmental income	532	617	688
5. Total federal	183	209	229
6. Civil federal	110	130	151
7. Military	73	78	78
8. State & local	349	408	459
9. Private income, not agricultural	3,387	3,796	4,132
10. Manufacturing	515	541	569
11. Mining	10	13	16
12. Contract construction	322	367	383
13. Public transportation & communication	588	662	725
14. Wholesale & retail commerce	813	925	1,000
15. Financing, Insurance, Real Estate	290	320	369
16. Services	837	956	1,055
17. Other income	11	12	14

The sectional distribution of the labor force matches, as is to be expected, the economic characteristics of the area. Of course, the ratio of jobs to product varies according to the economic activity and also according to the production techniques in use and the prices relative to the different production factors that contribute to the creation of a given economic benefit. We see that the service areas constitute the most important source of employment (representing 30 percent of the total) according to the *Manpower Area Planning Council's* report for 1970. Wholesale and retail activity is also very important, making up 23 percent of the total. This is followed by manufacturing which employs approximately 14 percent of the working force. The biggest changes noticed in the employment figures were in government, service areas, commerce, manufacturing, and the construction industry.

Following is an interesting comparative table of the rank of jobs not dealing with agriculture in Dade County and in the United States, and of the changes experienced at given periods of time.

RANK OF NON-AGRICULTURAL JOBS IN PERCENTAGES
OF THE TOTAL AND PERCENTAGES OF CHANGE

	Job Percentages Total by rank. 1958		1967		Percentage Changes in Total Employment by Rank 1958-1967	
	Dade	U.S.	Dade	U.S.	Dade	U.S.
Commerce	1	1	1	1	5	5
Services & Misc.	2	3	2	3	3	2
Manufacturing	3	4	3	4	2	1
Government	5	2	4	2	1	7
Public Transportation & Communication	4	7	5	7	6	3
Financing, Insurance, & Real Estate	7	5	6	5	4	8
Construction Contracts	6	6	7	6	7	6

Source: Department of Commerce for the State of Florida, Division of Labor. Employment Service of the State of Florida. *Labor Market Trends, 1947 to 1973* (Miami, Florida: Employment Office of the State of Florida, 1973).
Note: The discrepancies between this table and the data presented by M.A.P.C. as to the distribution of the labor force are due to the differences in defining and classifying the different economic areas under consideration.

Before continuing the description of the local economy, in particular that of the Hispanic Americans, one should ask, at least, what has been the impact produced by the Hispanic population growth on the rapid economic development of Dade County. The most specific influences produced have already been identified. Now we could make an evaluation of the economic effect that the population growth has produced.

Although it is bold to try to determine what the ideal population is for a given region or area, as this depends on a great number of factors, there is no doubt that the concept is important in planning the future development of the region. This is why presently there are vigorous debates on which line the county should follow in promoting the future development of the local economy. The estimated growth of the population is one of the most important variables in the evaluation of alternative courses of action.

Considering the recent past, it can be stated that the population growth of the sixties has made possible the high rate of economic development that has taken place, in the last decade and in this one, due to the combination of productive factors in Dade County during this period and the type of economic activities which have been favored. The population growth has served to stimulate, to act as a catalytic element for the economy of the county.

The population variable, together with other economic factors, has produced growth in all areas of the economy. This has been due primarily to an increase in the demand for goods and economic services, as well as for a vast range of public and social services. The population growth has brought with it a series of external economies which, as the dimension of the local economy expanded, have created a process of expansion and evolution in the structure of local activities. These reflect themselves in the types and degrees of changes registered on the matrix of the socio-economic activities in the area. To cite only a few examples, let us mention the rapid and steady growth in the following industries: transportation, communication, and public services; wholesale and retail commerce; general services, both professional and personal; financing, insurance, and real estate; the public sector; the construction industry; and last, general manufacturing, including food processing, the garment industry, lumber, furniture, metal products, paper, publications and printing, and transportation equipment.

Independent of the previous analysis, which has emphasized the indigenous factors that contributed to the economic growth, one should also underline, so as to make a balanced and accurate statement on the present and future of Dade County, the importance of all the activities related to the tourist industry. As the gross national product and, above all, the per capita income continue to increase in the United States (as measured in absolute figures even when the rate of growth of these indicators might drop at times), recreational activities and tourism will continue to expand.

To summarize, one can expect an evolution of the economic structure towards greater diversification and stability, although always noticeably influenced by tourist activities in which this area has a comparative advantage. This applies to national tourism specially from the east coast, as well as from Hispanic-American countries. This latter category has been growing rapidly in recent years. The final element of the economic structure of Miami will be the increasing importance given to commercial, financial, and cultural ties between this area and Hispanic America. If an active and decisive policy is followed in this field, its activities will become the basis of the local economy. Miami has the natural resources and the manpower for the task. These qualities give Miami a decisive superiority in relation to other areas of competition. In this sense, the

Characteristics and Consequences [151]

contribution that the Hispanic Americans make to local and national welfare will be much greater than in the past.

We have focused, although briefly, on the general and specific contributions that the Hispanic-American residents of the area have made to the economic success of Dade County. We will end this chapter with some data and descriptive comments on certain socio-economic aspects of the Hispanic population which are interesting per se as well as being important in the interpretation of future development.

A table of the percentage distribution of ethnic families and incomes for 1949, 1959, and 1969, comparing Dade County figures with thirty-three major cities in the country as presented in the *Standard Metropolitan Statistical Areas* follows:

PERCENTAGE OF FAMILIES AND INCOMES BY INCOME RANK

	\$5,000 or less		\$10,000 or less		\$15,000 or less	
	Families	Income	Families	Income	Families	Income
1969						
Total Dade County	24.1%	5.3%	45.4%	74.2%	21.5%	49.6%
White	19.6	4.5	48.9	76.6	23.7	52.0
Black	40.5	16.1	19.8	43.0	5.3	18.0
Hispanic Americans	24.5	6.9	35.5	61.4	12.5	32.0
1959						
Total Dade County	34.3	11.5	24.1	52.6	10.5	32.9
White	30.3	9.5	26.8	55.3	—	—
Non-white	63.9	41.3	4.4	12.5	—	—
1949						
Total Dade County	55.2	25.2	11.2	32.0	—	—
1969						
33 major SMSAs	14.9	3.6	55.5	78.8	26.4	51.0
White	12.4	2.9	59.2	80.9	28.8	53.1
Black	32.3	11.5	29.8	55.2	10.2	26.9

Sources: Census 1950, 1960, and 1970.

The previous table is interesting for it gives the relationship of income to dates and categories. The average Dade County family income by area or tracts in the 1970 census was \$9,241 for the total population, compared to \$8,091 for Hispanic families and \$5,979 for black families. The figures in the volume of the total income received by the Hispanic population today vary, depending on the source of information. The correct figures are probably somewhere between \$1.2 and \$1.5 billions.

In other statistical information, the Cuban families appear with an income figure higher than that of other Hispanic groups. An important contributing factor is the high percentage of Cuban women in the working force. These figures in 1972 were 54 percent compared to 42 percent for the total population and with even lower percentages for other Hispanic minorities. The income data closely correlates with the occupational distribution of the labor force.

The following table gives us a picture of the ethnic and racial characteristics of the working force in Dade County. The number of Hispanic American workers classified as skilled is very high. This compares well with E. H. Rogg's investigations (published 1970) in which the extraordinary concentration of Cubans in these categories can be clearly seen.

ETHNIC AND RACIAL CHARACTERISTICS OF THE LABOR FORCE
IN DADE COUNTY

	No. Black	% Employed	No. Hispanic American	% Employed	No. Balance	% Employed
Professional & Technical	4,719	6.6%	11,011	8.5%	52,936	16.9%
Managers & Administrators	1,497	2.1	7,481	5.7	37,807	12.1
Sales	1,608	2.3	9,013	6.9	34,189	10.9
Clerical	7,812	11.0	21,976	16.9	72,227	23.0
Specialized Workers	5,805	8.1	18,943	14.5	44,997	14.3
Operators	6,690	9.4	31,695	24.4	15,393	4.9
Transportation Workers	5,474	7.7	4,567	3.5	8,168	2.6
Manual Laborers	10,346	14.5	5,723	4.4	8,528	2.7
Agricultural Workers	1,876	2.6	1,105	0.8	1,823	0.6
Services	16,093	22.6	17,582	13.5	34,095	10.9
Domestic	9,319	13.1	1,114	0.9	1,552	0.5
Total	71,239	100.0	130,210	100.0	311,715	100.0

Source: "Profile of Metropolitan Dade County" C.I.P., 1970, p. 29.

Finally let us compare the 1966 income of Cubans living in the United States with their income in Cuba (in that same year) prior to exile. The concentration in the second classification is obvious.

RELATION BETWEEN THE INCOME OF THE REFUGEES IN CUBA AND IN DADE COUNTY IN 1966

	Monthly Family Gross Income in Cuba		
Monthly Family Gross Income in Miami	Less than $250	$250-450	$450-750
Less than $250	33.7%	25.3%	23.6%
$250 - 450	42.2	54.4	43.7
$450 - 750	15.6	15.2	27.7
More than $750	3.6	———	.8
Would Not Tell or Did Not Know	4.8	5.1	4.2

Source: Survey inquiry conducted by the Center of International Studies, University of Miami, July 1966. Tabulated by the Research Institute for Cuba and the Caribbean.

Although the relevant statistical information is not enough to arrive at positive conclusions, a comparison of this table to the onee howing istribution of family and total income for the various ethnic minorities, suggests to the writer that the differences in income between the total population and Hispanic Americans are lessening. The reasons are as follows: having passed some time as residents in the United States, the Hispanic Americans are more aware of the institutional and organizational functionings, as well as of the cultural forms and mechanisms of this society. This awareness allows them to act with greater efficiency in this environment. The acquisition of basic skills such as the speaking of English has also helped the Hispanic Americans to compete economically with more efficiency. As the professionals, technicians, and other specialized personnel have been able to reenter their former professions (this especially applies to Cubans), the inequality between the average income of the total population and that of the Hispanic Americans has diminished. Another favorable element is the steady increase of the number of firms in the hands of Hispanic Americans. Conservative figures estimate that more than 8,000 businesses in Dade County are owned by Hispanic Americans. Furthermore, the new generations which have been receiving their education in this country will face fewer difficulties in the labor market than their parents who came here as Cuban exiles. Dade County will become more and more a bilingual and bicultural area. This will be brought about not only by the huge local Hispanic American population, but also by the establishment and strengthening of the economic ties between Hispanic America and Southern Florida.

Some brief remarks also need to be made on the subject of unemployment. This is a problem of great importance to Dade County because of the effect it has had on economic growth during the past fifteen years.

The comparison of the unemployment indexes for Dade County and Florida and the nation, as well as those on total population, and the other study which does not include the refugees, shows an increase in local unemployment rates which coincide with the first stage of Cuban influx (1959-1962) and also with the economic recession in the United States in 1960-1961.

The rate of unemployment for Dade County was higher than that of the nation for 1960-1964, but maintained itself beneath the national rate up to 1972, the last year for which we have statistical comparisons. The unemployment studies, some of which include and others which exclude the Cuban refugee, show that from 1964 on there has been a gradual lessening of this classification until it has almost disappeared.

In my opinion, these facts substantiate the general impressions on the economic growth process of the area stated at the beginning of this chapter. The gradual formation and strengthening of a new market, characterized by expansion of production, income, and employment in a classical growth process of increase in productivity and decrease in production costs, are the results of population increase and competitive business practices. This has brought about the final absorption of the new labor force. The new supply created a new demand. It should be added, without taking any merit away from this perhaps unique human effort, that the Hispanic Americans have enjoyed a double and partially contradictory advantage in this saga. The first is that, at their arrival, they found a socioeconomic infrastructure typical of the highest developed society in the world, one which is exceptionally rich on a per capita basis. Second, is the fact that although Dade County's economy was already at a high income level in the beginning of the last decade, it was not characterized by the technical complexity normal for an economy of this magnitude.

In conclusion, this summary should not give us a satisfactory feeling of accomplishment. The surveys seem to show that Hispanic-American unemployment has increased disproportionately, in relation to the total population, especially if compared to the non-Hispanic white segments of the community, We will not analyze this phenomenon at this time. There are many reasons for it, and any conclusion drawn from the unemployment rate of the Hispanic-American minority involves problems of measurement due to the various definitions of unemployment, cultural characteristics, and statistical procedures. This does not mean that the problem does not exist. It is real and very important. Every kind of effort should be made to resolve this serious situation.

In this chapter I have tried to point out only that a lessening of the unemployment problem is intimately linked to the adoption of a series of measures that would assure the continuous economic expansion of this area. Without going into these measurements, I will limit myself to indicating the desired result. This would be the steady growth of the local economy in complete cooperation and harmony and with true opportunities for all. The full use of resources at our disposal requires the participation and help of all the population in the delicate task of mixing cultures and efforts in an internationally oriented cosmopolitan environment. It will need the practice of policies and preparatory programs that will facilitate the integration of the diverse segments of the population in a common effort that will benefit all.

The Hispanic contribution to the economy of Miami in the past fifteen years has been very important. It can be more so in the future if we work together for the general good.

INDEX

Abercromby, Gen. Sir Ralph, 20
Acosta, José de, 67
Adams, John, 22, 98
Adams, John Quincy, 27
Adams, Samuel, 25, 107
Agüeybana, 39, 40
Aguilar, Marcos de, 39, 43
Aguilera, F. V., 135
Aguirre, Dr. Horacio, 17, 139
Alaminos, Antón de, 48, 49
Aldama, 135
Alegria, Dr. Ricardo E., 19
Alfaro, Colón Eloy, 17
Alfaro, Ricardo, 17
Altamira, Rafael, 17
Añasco, Luis de, 40
Angeles, Victoria de los, 10
Anglería Pedro Mártir de, 50, 54
Aragón, Ernesto de, 16
Arango, Sancho de, 40
Arrau, Claudio, 10
Artigas, José, 25
Ashburn, Dr. D. P. M., 86
Avila, Gil González de, 40
Ayllón, Luis Vasquez de, 67

Balboa, Vasco Núñez de, 51
Balseiro, José Agustín, 14
Balseiro, Mercedes P. de, 13, 31
Balseiro, (Dávila) Rafael, 10
Bancroft, George, 127
Barasorda, Antonio, 140
Barcia, Andrés Gonzáles, 87
Bartram, William, 99
Batista, Fulgencio, 135
Beaumarchais, Pierre Caron de, 22
Belaval, Emilio, Jr., 140n
Bello, Andrés, 25
Bemis, S. F., 101, 116

Benavides, Gov. Antonio de, 88
Bennett, Charles E., 108
Bermúdez, Diego, 48
Blaine, James G., 129, 130
Blanco, Andrés Eloy, 16
Bolet brothers (A. and J.), 10
Bolívar, Simón, 25, 26, 27, 31, 105
Bono de Quejo, Juan, 35, 38, 43, 48
Botkin, B. A., 74
Boyd, Mark, 110, 111, 112
Burgoyne, Gen. John, 22

Cabeya de Vaca, Alvar Núñez, 17, 30, 67
Caboto, Sebastián, 50, 51, 58
Cabrera, Gov. Juan Marqués, 81, 84, 89
Cagigal, Gen. Juan Manuel, 18, 19, 20, 105
Calancha, 86
Calhoun, John C., 27
Camín, Alfonso, 13, 16
Campbell, Brig. Archibald, 109, 110
Camprubí, Zenobia, 11, 12, 16
Cansyno, García, 40
Capron, L., 68
Cárdenas, Pedro de, 38
Cardona, Francisco de, 38, 42
Carlos I. *See* Charles I
Carlos II. *See* Charles II
Carrión, Dr. Arturo Morales, 19
Caruso, John Anthony, 100, 103
Casas, Bartolomé de las, 36, 42
Castro, Alvarez de, 67
Castro, Américo, 13
Castro, Capt. Gen. Ramón de, 20
Castro, Fidel, 135
Catherine II of Russia, 18, 21
Cea, Alonzo de, 38
Cerda, Gasper de la, 11
Cerón, Juan, 35, 36, 37, 38, 40, 41, 43
Cervantes, Miguel de, 27

[157]

Chapuz, Miguel Josef, 111
Charles I (Emperor), 13, 58, 82
Charles II (Emperor), 18, 21, 100
Chester, Peter, 100, 103
Chichi-Okobee, 74
Cisneros, Cardinal Francisco Ximénez, 36, 42, 53, 55
Clarke, J., 146
Clay, Henry, 27
Clement (Clemente) VII (pope), 19
Cleveland, Grover, 130, 131
Clinton, Gen. Henry, 103
Columbus, Christopher (Colón, Cristóbal), 35, 45, 48, 53, 56, 133
Colón, Bartolomé, 48
Colón, Cristóbal. *See* Columbus, Christopher
Colón, Diego, 35, 36, 37, 38, 39, 40, 43, 44, 48, 51, 52, 57
Commager, Henry S., 109
Conchillos, 42
Cooper, Peter, 124
Cornwallis, Gen. Charles, 20, 112
Cortés, Hernán, 58

Dann, Carl, 75
Darío, Rubén, 29
Dávila, Dr. José Antonio, 10
Dávila, Pedrarías, 54
Dávila, Raúl, 140n
Davis, John (alias Robert Searles), 79, 81, 82, 84
Densmore, F., 68
Deveaux, Col. Andrew, 116
Deymier, Aida, 31
Díaz, Justino, 140n
Díaz, Miguel, 35, 36, 37, 38, 39, 40, 41
Doering, J. F., 73
Drake, Sir Francis, 78

Egaña, Juan, 25
Elvas, 66
Elvira, Pablo, 140n
Emerson, Ralph Waldo, 27, 124
Enrique, Captain, 43
Escalera, Nicolás de la, 138
Escobar, Vicente, 138
Escobedo, Alonso Gregorio, 11
Estebanillo, 20
Estenós, Gov. Ramírez de, 20

Fernando (king of Spain), 35-60
Ferré, Antonio, 16
Ferré, Mayor Maurice A., 9, 16
Fish, Jesse, 120
Floridablanca, Francisco, 101, 102, 103
Fonseca, Bishop Rodríguez de, 50
Fontaneda, Hernando Escalante, 67
Franklin, Benjamin, 20, 22, 23, 24, 27, 29, 30, 116, 117, 126, 127, 128, 130, 131
Freeman, Mrs. Joseph, 31
Frisonou, Dr. Juan, 88

Gallatin, Albert, 30
Gallegos, Rómulo, 16
Gálvez, Bernardo de, 18, 22, 103, 104, 105, 110, 111, 112, 116, 117
Gálvez, José de, 103
Gama, Antonio de la, 42, 56, 57
Garay, Francisco, 58

García Lorca, Federico, 12, 140n
Garcilaso de la Vega, "The Inca," 11, 33, 50, 67
Garnet, Henry, 124
Germana (wife of Fernando), 39
Ginorio, Rosita, 140n
Gladstone, William, 24
Gomara, Lope de, 55
Gómez de Avillaneda, Gertrudis, 26
González, Fr. Juan, 57
Gorham, Nathaniel, 127
Grana, Josefina de la, 70
Grant, Gov. James, 106, 107, 113
Grant, Ulysses S., 27
Grasse, Joseph Paul de, 19, 105, 106
Griffis, Stanton, 18
Juerra, Gov. Francisco de la, 81

Hamilton, Alexander, 23, 30, 127, 130
Hanna, Kathryn Abbey, 105, 107, 110
Haro, Andrés de, 54
Harvey, Adm. Henry, 20
Hauptmann, C. H., 72
Hay, John, 22
Hayne, Robert, 24
Hemingway, Ernest, 10
Henry VIII (king of England), 51
Henry, Patrick, 25
Heredia, José Mariá, 134, 135
Hernández-Catá family, 16
Hernández, Dr. Francisco, 85
Herrera, Antonio de, 33, 34, 49, 50
Herrera, Luciano de, 111
Heyward, Thomas Jr., 113
Holmes, Jack D. L., 96
Howard, Clinton N., 100
Howe, Gen. Robert, 109, 111
Howe, Gen. William, 108
Hugo, Victor, 125

Ibáñez, Carlos, 13
Ibarra, Gov. Pedro de, 84
Iturbi, Amparo, 10
Iturbi, José, 10

Jackson, Andrew, 130
Jackson, W. R., Jr., 66
Jay, John, 118
Jefferson, Thomas, 22, 23, 24, 25, 27, 29, 30, 126, 130, 131
Jiménez, Juan Ramón, 11, 12, 13, 16
Johnson, Cecil, 100
Johnstone, Gov. George, 99, 100, 106, 107
Joijo, Maria, 82
Jorge, 30
Juan II (king of Portugal), 45

Kennedy, S., 72
King, Rufus, 30
Kynerd, B. A., 99

Laredo, Jaime, 10
Lawson, Edward W., 59
Layfayette, Marquis de, 22, 32n
LeConte, Juan de, 80, 81, 88
Lecuona, Ernesto, 10
Lee, Robert E., 27
Le Moyne, 88

Index

Leslie, John, 120
Lewis, Charles Lee, 19
Lincoln, Abraham, 24, 27, 29
Lizaso, Félix, 28
Lizaur, Francisco de, 36, 37, 38, 39, 41, 42
Longfellow, Henry Wadsworth, 124
Lopez, Narciso, 135
Lopez de Cárdenas, Garcia, 17
Lopez de Toledo, Capt. Sebastian, 87
Louis XVI (king of France), 22
Ludwig, Emil, 125
Lummis, Charles F., 17

Maceo, 135
Machado, Antonio, 12
Machado, Gerardo, 135
Madison, James, 23, 27, 127, 130
Magellan, 47, 51
Makarova, Natalia, 137
Maldonado, Cristóbal, 56
Mañach, Jorge, 28
Manso, Bishop Alonso, 43
Manuel (king of Portugal), 44, 47, 52, 53
Martel, Pérez, 57
Martí, José, 10, 27, 28, 29, 123-132, 134, 135
Martínez, Gov. Domingo, 86
Martir, Pedro, 67
Marx, Karl, 127
Matienzo, Dr., 55
McLean, Irene, 140n
Melgarejo, Diego, 57
Méndez de Canzo, Gov. Gonzalo, 78, 83, 84
Menéndez, Catalina, 83
Menéndez de Avilés, Pedro, 9, 14, 17, 62, 66, 77, 80
Menéndez Marqués, Francisco, 85
Menéndez Marqués, Gov. Pedro, 80, 81, 83, 86
Menendez Pidal, Ramón, 12
Mercadal, Juan, 140n
Middleton, Arthur, 113
Mir, 140n
Miranda, Francisco de, 18-22, 105, 106, 112, 116
Miruelo, Diego, 48, 49
Mistral, Gabriela, 12
Mistral, Nati, 137
Monardes, Dr. Nicolás, 85-88
Montalvo, Juan, 27
Monteverde, Domingo, 21
Montoya, Carlos, 140n
Moore, Gov. James, 79, 85
Morales, Andrés, 52
Morales, Diego de, 35, 36
Morales, Lemus, 135
Moreno, García, 27
Moreno de Alba, Dr. Francisco, 89
Morison, Samuel Eliot, 127
Morris, A. C., 76
Morris, Gouverneur, 127
Moscoso, Rodrigo de, 43, 48
Mowat, Charles Loch, 107, 108, 109

Nagy, Ivan, 137
Napoleon, 26
Narváez, Pónfilo de, 17, 62
Navarro de la Torre, José, 110, 111, 112
Neruda, Pablo, 12
Niza, Fr. Marcos de, 30

North, Lord, 116
Nuceti-Sardi, Juan, 106

Olmedo, José Joaquin, 26
O'Neill, Arturo, 106
Oré, Fr. Gerónimo de, 13, 33
Ortubia, Juan Perez de, 48, 49, 51
Osceola, 62
Ovando, Fr. Nicolás de, 36, 37, 41, 57
Oviedo, Hernández de, 67

Pacheco, Emilio, 28
Paine, Thomas, 25, 31, 105, 126
Palmer, Courtlandt, 124
Panton, William, 120
Pasamonte, Miguel de, 42, 44, 45, 46, 48, 50, 51
Paterson, William, 127
Pennington, Edgar Legarde, 108
Pereira, Dr. Octavio Méndez, 17
Pineda, Juana de, 57
Pinzón, Vicente Yañez, 45, 46, 47, 48, 50, 51, 53
Phillip II (Emperor), 13, 83
Phillips, Wendell, 124
Piques, Pedro, 81
Pitt, William, 21
Polk, James, 27
Ponce, Hernán, 59
Ponce de León, Cristóbal, 57
Ponce de León, Ens. Francisco, 88
Ponce de León, Francisca, 34, 58
Ponce de León, Isabel, 57
Ponce de León, Juan, 5, 17, 30, 33-60, 62, 66, 67
Ponce de León, Juan Troche, 59
Ponce de León, Juan II, 59
Ponce de León, Juana, 57
Ponce de León, Leonor, 57
Ponce de León, Luis, 57
Ponce de León, Maria, 57
Prevost, Brig. Gen. Augustine, 110
Puente, Josef Elixio de la, 111, 112
Puente, Juan Elixio de la, 111, 112

Quevedo, Francisco de, 70

Randolph, Edmund, 127
Rebolledo, Gov. Diego de, 86
Regoyas, Dario, 140n
Remos, Dr. Juan J., 140n
Rey, Carlos del, 88
Rivera, Graciela, 10
Robertson, Piedad F., 9n, 33n, 141n
Robertson, William S., 21, 31
Robespierre, 127
Robson, Carlos, 81
Rockingham, Marquis of, 116
Rogg, E. H., 152
Roig, Gonzalo, 137
Romero, Gil, 38
Ronsal, Stephan, 19
Rutledge, Edward, 113

Saco, José Antonio, 134, 135
Saint-Simon, 19
Salazar, Capt., 40
Salinas, Pedro, 12
San Martin, Gen., 20

Sanromá, Jesús Maria, 10
Sarmiento, Faustino Domingo, 26, 125
Schuyler, R. L., 25
Sedeño, Antonio de, 58
Segovia, Andrés, 10, 140n
Segovia, Hernando de, 82
Shelburne, Lord, 116, 117
Siebert, Wilbur H., 115
Sigüenza y Gongora, Carlos de, 11
Simón, Dr. José, 19, 31n
Solana, Fr. Juan José, 85
Solís, Humberto, 141n
Solís, Juan de, 45, 46, 47, 48, 50, 51, 52, 53
Sorolla, 140n
Soto, Hernando de, 11, 17, 74
Sotomayer, Cristóbal de, 39, 40
Sotomayer party, 43, 54
Sotomayor, Pedro, 40
Sparks, J. M. Jared, 19
Stuart, Col. John, 99, 100

Tapia, Cristóbal de, 58
Thoreau, Henry David, 26
Thorning, J. F., 106
Tió, Aurelio, 19
Tonyn, Gov. Patrick, 107, 108, 109, 110, 113-114, 119-120
Troche, García, 37, 42, 55, 56, 57, 58
Troche, Gaspar, 57
Troche, Leonor, 57
Torroba, Federico Moreno, 137
Truman, Harry S., 31
Trussell, Mr., 75

Unamuno, Miguel de, 27

Vaca de Osma, José Antonio, 18
Vallejo, Antonio Buero, 140n
Vallejo, Governor, 59
Varela, Fr. Félix, 134, 135
Vasconcillos, Méndez, 47
Veintimilla, Ignacio, 27
Velasco, López de, 67
Velázquez, Diego, 55, 59
Velázquez, Francisco, 55
Velázquez, Sancho, 37, 41, 42, 56
Vergil, 70
Vespucio, Américo (Amerigo Vespucci), 44, 46, 50, 51
Vespucio, Juan, 44, 46, 51
Villa-Lobos, Heitor, 10
Villaverde, 135

Washington, George, 19, 21, 23, 24, 25, 26, 27, 29, 30, 127, 130, 131
Webster, Daniel, 24, 27, 130
Webster, Noah, 25
Whitaker, Arthur Preston, 118, 119
Whitman, Walt, 124
Willing, James, 103
Wilson, James, 127
Woodward, Dr. Henry, 82

Ybor, Vicente Martínez, 63
Yela Utrillo, J. F., 115

Zambrana, Dr., 29
Zapatero, Juan Manuel, 96
Zenea, Juan Clemente, 135
Zespedes, Gov. Manuel, 120
Zúñiga, Iñigo de, 38, 41, 42